Twayne's United States Authors Series

EDITOR OF THIS VOLUME

Kenneth E. Eble

University of Utah

Pearl S. Buck

Revised Edition

TUSAS 85

Pearl S. Buck

PEARL S. BUCK

REVISED EDITION

By PAUL A. DOYLE

Nassau Community College,
State University of New York

TWAYNE PUBLISHERS
A DIVISION OF G. K. HALL & CO., BOSTON

Library of Congress Cataloging in Publication Data

Doyle, Paul A
Pearl S. Buck.
(Twayne's United States authors series ; TUSAS 85)
Bibliography: p. 168-75
Includes index.
1. Buck, Pearl Sydenstricker, 1892-1973—Criticism
and interpretation.
PS3503.U198Z64   1980   813'.52   80-24376
ISBN 0-8057-7325-8

Contents

About the Author

Preface

Acknowledgments

Chronology

1. Two Worlds Interacting 15

2. *The Good Earth* 29

3. Fame That Was Not Fleeting 42

4. The Nobel Prize Biographies 67

5. The Nobel Aura 77

6. Popular Novels and the War Crusade 94

7. Perspectives of East and West 113

8. A Humanitarian As Well 129

9. Novels of the Last Decade 137

10. A Final Reckoning 148

Notes and References 155

Selected Bibliography 168

Index 176

About the Author

Dr. Paul A. Doyle is author or editor of fourteen books including *A Concordance to the Collected Poems of James Joyce*; *Sean O'Faolain*; and *Liam O'Flaherty* (both in the Twayne English Authors Series); *Paul Vincent Carroll: A Critical Introduction; Henry David Thoreau: Studies and Commentaries*; *Guide to Basic Information Sources in English Literature*; *Evelyn Waugh: A Checklist of Primary and Secondary Material*; *Liam O'Flaherty: An Annotated Bibliography*.

Dr. Doyle has published articles in over sixty different journals and periodicals including *South Atlantic Quarterly, James Joyce Quarterly, Twentieth Century Literature, English Journal, Dublin Review, American Speech, Renascence, Walt Whitman Review, English Literature in Transition, Papers of the Bibliographical Society of America, Eire-Ireland, Four Quarters*, etc.

He is the editor of the *Nassau Review* and Chief of the Editorial Board of the *Evelyn Waugh Newsletter*. He is a Research Consultant for *English Literature in Transition*, and reviews books for several periodicals.

He has taught at various colleges and is presently Professor of English at Nassau Community College, State University of New York.

Preface

The manuscript of the first edition of this book was accepted in 1963; consequently, no analysis of Pearl Buck's later novels could be included. This new edition, therefore, analyzes the principal novels of her last decade beginning with *The Living Reed*. Pearl Buck wrote and published steadily until March 6, 1973, the day of her death, and also left several posthumous works, mainly short stories.

In addition to completing an analysis of the corpus of her work, I have brought the bibliography up to date, noted post-1963 research and criticism, and made several revisions and additions throughout. Emphasis has again been placed on her novels as well as those nonfiction materials that are most significant and best illuminate her point of view. Necessary biographical and general background has also been given in order to place her writings and attitudes in total perspective.

I was astounded by the voluminous amount of correspondence from all over the world that favorably greeted the first edition. The letters attested to Pearl Buck's continued popularity (even now she remains the most widely translated author in the history of American literature) and often sought more data. I would recommend that readers of this new edition peruse carefully the notes and references where many details about Buck's views, short stories, plays, etc., are included and documented in order to prevent the main text from becoming overly detailed and digressive. Many of the questions I have been asked are answered in the notes which deliberately have been made extensive.

I have, further, tried to reach a more balanced position toward Pearl Buck's writing. Her work does not deserve the disdain that many literary pundits have heaped upon it. On the other hand, her books do not merit the uncritical adulation that they have often received.

There can be no question that her reputation as a writer suffered somewhat for two reasons which are shameful. First, she has been unduly deprecated at times because she was a woman writer and, especially, a woman Nobel Prize winner. Secondly, she has often been denigrated because so much of her work deals with Chinese and Asiatic materials. This focus has caused some American critics and reviewers to regard her as really a foreign writer whose work must be, ipso facto, in their view, of secondary interest.

I must again thank Miss Margaret Thomas of the Lipscomb Library of Randolph-Macon Woman's College and Miss Dorothy W. Bridgwater of the Yale University Reference Department. Special gratitude is expressed to Dr. Cecilia Chen, Miss Daphne Atkinson, and Mr. John A. Shade, Jr., the Executive Director of the Pearl S. Buck Foundation. I thank Professor Joanna Poletti and Dr. Dorothea R. Walker, valued colleagues at Nassau Community College, and Editor Sandra Conrad of the *Bulletin of Bibliography* for supplying useful references. My appreciation is also extended to the librarians at Nassau College, especially Mr. Emanuel Finkel, Mrs. Edith Forbes, Mrs. Vera Jerwick, Mrs. Jean Mancuso, Mrs. Aurelia Stephan, Mrs. Doris Victor, and Mrs. Mildred White.

Many librarians and their institutions were especially cooperative in helping to furnish information about Pearl S. Buck and to procure her letters and documents. Particular appreciation is expressed to those in charge of collections at the following libraries: Allegheny College Library; Allentown (Penna.) Free Library; Berea College Library; Colby College Library; Baker Library, Dartmouth College; Duke University Library; Harvard University Library; Haverford College Library; Historical Society of Pennsylvania; Newark Public Library; The Newberry Library; New York Public Library; Pack Memorial Public Library, Asheville, N.C.; State Historical Society of Wisconsin; Vassar College Library; University of Virginia Library.

PAUL A. DOYLE

Nassau Community College,
State University of New York
Garden City, Long Island

Acknowledgments

I wish to express my gratitude to the following for permission to quote from copyrighted material:

To Pearl S. Buck, to the Graduate Department of Yale University, and to Yale University Library for permission to quote from Buck's personal letters deposited in the Yale Library.

To the John Day Company, Inc., grateful acknowledgment is made for permission to use throughout this volume quotations from the following copyrighted works of Pearl S. Buck: *A Bridge for Passing, A House Divided, American Argument, American Triptych, American Unity and Asia, The Chinese Novel, Command the Morning, Dragon Seed, The Exile, Fighting Angel, Friend to Friend, God's Men, The Good Earth, Is There A Case for the Foreign Missions?, Kinfolk, The Mother, My Several Worlds, Of Men and Women, Other Gods, The Patriot, Pavilion of Women, The Promise, Sons, This Proud Heart, The Townsman,* and *What America Means to Me.*

To the American Academy of Arts and Letters for permission to quote from the Academy's *Proceedings* (1953).

To Atheneum Publishers for permission to quote from Kenneth Tynan, *Curtains,* copyright © 1961 by Kenneth Tynan.

To Melville H. Cane, executor of Sinclair Lewis's will, for permission to quote from an address given by Lewis at a gathering of the American Pen Club.

To Coward-McCann, Inc., for permission to reprint material from *The Exile's Daughter* by Cornelia Spencer. Copyright © 1944 by Coward-McCann, Inc.

To James Gray and the University of Minnesota Press for permission to quote from James Gray, *On Second Thought* (1946).

To Harper & Row, Publishers, Inc., for permission to quote from *The Goddess Abides* by Pearl S. Buck. Copyright © 1972 by Creativity, Inc., and from *The Woman Who Was Changed and Other Stories* by Pearl S. Buck. Copyright © 1979 by The Pearl S. Buck Foundation.

To Harcourt, Brace & World, Inc., for permission to quote from E. M. Forster, *Aspects of the Novel* (1927).

To the National Council of Teachers of English for permission to quote from Phyllis Bentley, "The Art of Pearl S. Buck," *English Journal* (December, 1935).

To the *New Republic* for permission to quote from Malcolm Cowley's review of *The Patriot* (May 10, 1939) and from Younghill Kang's review of *The Good Earth* (July 1, 1931).

To the *New York Times* for permission to quote from Brooks Atkinson's review of *A Desert Incident* (March 25, 1959) and from Charles Poore's review of *Kinfolk* (April 21, 1949).

To Elizabeth Janeway and the *New York Times* for permission to quote from Mrs. Janeway's review of *The Hidden Flower* (May 25, 1952).

To Macmillan Publishing Company, Inc., for permission to quote from Oscar Cargill, *Intellectual America: Ideas on the March* (1941); from *Literary History of the United States,* ed. Robert Spiller, et al., (1948); and from Carl Van Doren, *The American Novel: 1789-1939*, revised edition (1940).

To University of Oklahoma Press for permission to quote from *Nobel: The Man and His Prizes*, ed. Nobel Foundation (1951).

To Oxford University Press for permission to quote from James D. Hart, *The Popular Book* (1950).

To *Saturday Review* for permission to quote from Henry Seidel Canby, "*The Good Earth*: Pearl Buck and the Nobel Prize" (November 19, 1938).

To *Scientific American* for permission to quote from V. S. Pritchett's review of *Command the Morning* (July, 1959).

To The Viking Press for permission to quote from J. Donald Adams, *The Shape of Books to Come* (1944) and from James Joyce, *A Portrait of the Artist as a Young Man* (Viking Compass Book).

To Edmund Wilson and his publisher Farrar, Straus & Cudahy, Inc., for permission to quote from Edmund Wilson, *Classics and Commercials* (1950).

Chronology

1892   Pearl Buck born on June 26, in Hillsboro, West Virginia, while her parents—Absalom and Caroline (Stulting) Sydenstricker—were on furlough from their missionary activities in China. Taken to China as an infant.

1900   Family forced to flee to Shanghai during Boxer Rebellion.

1909   Sent to boarding school in Shanghai.

1910   Went to America to enter Randolph-Macon Woman's College, Lynchburg, Virginia.

1914   Received bachelor of arts from Randolph-Macon Woman's College. Accepted an assistantship at the college and began to teach, but soon returned to China to take care of her ill mother.

1917   May 13, married in China to John Lossing Buck, an American agricultural specialist. She and her husband went to live in North China.

1921   Moved to Nanking where her husband taught agricultural theory at the university.

1921–   Taught English literature at the University of Nanking. Also
1931   taught irregularly at Southeastern University, Nanking, 1925–27; at Chung Yang University in Nanking, 1928–30.

1925   Came to America. Studied at Cornell.

1926   Received master of arts degree in English from Cornell University; returned to China.

1927   Barely escaped alive during a revolutionary army attack on Nanking.

1930   *East Wind: West Wind.*

1931   *The Good Earth.*

1932   Won Pulitzer Prize for *The Good Earth. The Young Revolutionist. Sons.*

1933   *The First Wife and Other Stories. All Men Are Brothers* (translation of *Shui Hu Chuan*).

1934   *The Mother.* Decided to take up permanent residence in the United States.

1935 *A House Divided. House of Earth (The Good Earth, Sons, A House Divided*—trilogy published in one volume). Divorced from John Lossing Buck. June 11, married Richard J. Walsh, president of the John Day publishing firm. November, awarded the William Dean Howells medal by the American Academy of Arts and Letters, presented for the finest work of American fiction within the years 1930–35.

1936 Elected to membership in The National Institute of Arts and Letters. *The Exile. Fighting Angel.*

1938 *This Proud Heart.* Won Nobel Prize in Literature.

1939 *The Patriot. The Chinese Novel. Flight into China* (play produced in September 1939).

1940 *Other Gods. Stories for Little Children.*

1941 *Today and Forever. Of Men and Women* (reprinted with new epilogue, 1971). Founded the East and West Association, a nonprofit group desiring to bring about greater understanding among the peoples of the world.

1942 *Dragon Seed. American Unity and Asia. The Chinese Children Next Door* (book for children). *China Sky.*

1943 *What America Means to Me. The Water-Buffalo Children* (book for children). *The Promise. Twenty-Seven Stories* (contains all the stories published in *The First Wife and Other Stories* and *Today and Forever*).

1944 *The Spirit and the Flesh (The Exile* and *Fighting Angel* published together in one volume). *The Dragon Fish* (book for children). *The Story of Dragon Seed.*

1945 *Tell the People* (in collaboration with James Yen). *The Townsman* (under pseudonym John Sedges). *Yu-Lan: Flying Boy of China* (book for children). *Talk About Russia* (in collaboration with Masha Scott). *The First Wife* (play produced in November 1945). *Portrait of a Marriage. China Flight.* Edited *China in Black and White: An Album of Woodcuts by Contemporary Chinese Artists.*

1946 *Pavilion of Women.*

1947 *How It Happens: Talk about the German People, 1914–1933* (in collaboration with Erna von Pustau). *The Angry Wife* (under pseudonym John Sedges). *Far and Near: Stories of Japan, China, and America.*

1948 *The Big Wave* (book for children). *Peony.*

1949 *American Argument* (in collaboration with Eslanda Goode Robeson). *Kinfolk. The Long Love* (under pseudonym John

Sedges). Founded Welcome House, an adoption agency for Asian-American children.

1950   *The Child Who Never Grew. One Bright Day* (book for children).

1951   *God's Men.*

1952   *The Hidden Flower. Bright Procession* (under pseudonym John Sedges).

1953   *Voices in the House* (under pseudonym John Sedges). *Come, My Beloved. The Man Who Changed China: The Story of Sun Yat-sen* (book for children).

1954   *The Beech Tree* (book for children). *Johnny Jack and His Beginnings* (book for children). *My Several Worlds.*

1956   *Imperial Woman.*

1957   *Letter from Peking. Christmas Miniature* (book for children). *My Several Worlds* (abridged for younger readers).

1958   *American Triptych* (containing three John Sedges novels: *The Townsman, Voices in the House, The Long Love*). *Friend to Friend* (in collaboration with Carlos Romulo).

1959   *A Desert Incident* (play produced in March 1959). *Command the Morning.*

1960   Coauthor of *Christine*, a musical produced in April 1960. *The Christmas Ghost* (book for children).

1961   *Fourteen Stories.*

1962   *Satan Never Sleeps* (a movie script written by Buck from an outline by Leo McCarey; published as a paperback novel). *A Bridge for Passing. Hearts Come Home and Other Stories* (contains stories selected from *The First Wife and Other Stories, Far and Near*, and one story from *Today and Forever*).

1963   *The Living Reed.*

1964   *Welcome Child* (book for children). *The Joy of Children. Stories of China* (an omnibus volume containing the short stories formerly published in *The First Wife and Other Stories* and *Today and Forever*). Established the Pearl S. Buck Foundation to care for children of half-American parentage who have been born in Asian countries and live in these countries.

1965   *Death in the Castle*. Edited *Fairy Tales of the Orient. The Guide* (a play adapted from the novel by N. K. Narayan). *Children for Adoption. The Gifts They Bring: Our Debt to the Mentally Retarded* (in collaboration with Gweneth T. Zarfoss). *The Big Fight* (book for children). *My Mother's House* (in collaboration with others).

1966　*For Spacious Skies: Journey in Dialogue* (in collaboration with Theodore F. Harris). *The People of Japan. The Little Fox in the Middle* (book for children).

1967　*The Time Is Noon. To My Daughters, With Love. Matthew, Mark, Luke, and John* (book for children).

1968　*The New Year.*

1969　*The Good Deed and Other Stories of Asia, Past and Present. The Three Daughters of Madame Liang.*

1970　*China as I See It* (edited by Theodore F. Harris). *The Kennedy Women: A Personal Approach. Mandala.*

1971　*The Story Bible. The Chinese Story Teller* (book for children). *Pearl Buck's America.*

1972　*The Goddess Abides. China: Past and Present. A Community Success Story* (in collaboration with Elisabeth Waechter). *Once Upon a Christmas* (stories for young adults). *Pearl Buck's Oriental Cookbook.*

1973　Died March 6 of lung cancer at her "second home" in Danby, Vermont. Buried at Green Hills Farm, her Perkasie, Pa., estate. This farm is now a National Historic Site and the International Headquarters of the Pearl S. Buck Foundation. *All Under Heaven. A Gift for the Children* (book for children). *Mrs. Starling's Problem* (book for children).

1974　*The Rainbow. Words of Love* (poems). Edited *Pearl S. Buck's Book of Christmas.*

1975　*East and West.*

1976　*Mrs. Stoner and the Sea, and Other Works. Secrets of the Heart.*

1977　*The Lovers and Other Stories.*

1979　*The Woman Who Was Changed and Other Stories.*

CHAPTER 1

Two Worlds Interacting

I N one of her very last novels Pearl S. Buck emphasized a classical phrase from ancient Chinese literature: "All under heaven are one."[1] She had known two worlds—the world of her American missionary parents and the world of a continually fascinating Orient. She was in the curious position of existing "in one world and not of it, and belonging to another world and yet not of it."[2] Nevertheless, she continually attempted to bridge both worlds; she "belonged as much to the one as to the other."[3] Even when her two worlds came to a more definite division at the time when she chose to settle permanently in the United States, she never left her other existence far behind.

Although the Communists were especially hostile to her and her writings, she welcomed the President Nixon initiative which brought new American and Chinese ties. It was one of her deepest regrets that the Red Chinese government would not grant her a visa during this more amiable period. Yet she could, throughout her life, truly assert: "It would be hard for me to declare which side of the world is most my own. . . . I am loyal to Asia as I am loyal to my own land."[4] Less than a year before she died, she lovingly called China "my other country." Buck has given her writing and thinking additional meaning and dimension by observing matters from two perspectives. Her background and her experience enable her to possess a two-sided view of every situation. Both as a person and as a writer, the worlds of East and West have broadened her spiritually and increased her depth of understanding and sympathy. The East and the West meet in her and bring a mature realization of both differences and similarities, and this realization becomes a hallmark of her vision of life. She is the intermediary between two worlds and two cultures.

I   *Early Years*

Although born in the United States, Pearl Sydenstricker when only a few months old was taken to China by her missionary parents.[5] There she was reared and spent her early, formative years. China stamped itself indelibly on the young child's mind and imagination. China was an exotic world—in itself worthy of a storybook: a world of quaint tiled roofs, Buddhist temples, strange but impressive statues of unknown gods, and colorful, unusual festival celebrations. China contained an infinite variety of people ranging from destitute beggars and picturesque, venerable elders to uncivilized bandits in the nearby hills who often raided the towns and hamlets. Pearl Sydenstricker's father and mother always disdained the forbidding and aloof mission compounds; they preferred to live and work among the native populace. Thus the young child grew up in close intimacy with the Chinese people. She spoke Chinese, played with Chinese children, visited them in their homes, listened to their ideas, and came to know their feelings and viewpoints.

The young girl was obsessed with stories. She admits that she was "a curious child plaguing everyone with questions sometimes too intimate and personal."[6] A story about anyone near or far intrigued her, but she was especially interested in the lives of people about her. She remembers that she listened hour after hour to anyone who would talk to her, and she notes that the Chinese were not reticent about discussing at length their own lives.

In particular, the young Pearl Sydenstricker listened to an almost endless series of stories related by her old Chinese nurse, and she later declared that this was the first literary influence she received.[7] This Chinese amah was especially fond of narrating Buddhist and Taoist legends. The Buddhist stories intrigued the American child with their imaginative flights—such as in the tale about strange daggers which could be so diminished in size as to be hidden in an ear or in the corner of one's eye, but which, when held for battle or defense, could become long and powerful. The Taoist stories concerned devils, fairies, and fantastic spirits who lived in stones and trees, and dragons who dwelt in winds and storm.

In addition to the marvelous tales told by the Chinese amah, Pearl Sydenstricker heard unusual and intriguing stories from her father. As a missionary, Absalom Sydenstricker traveled to remote regions of the country and had experienced many rare, exciting, and hazardous adventures. Although he was by nature inclined to be reserved and reticent, he related, upon his return, some of his adventures and experiences; and these episodes deeply impressed his young daughter.

Caroline Sydenstricker, Pearl's mother, was a born raconteur and entertainer. Mrs. Sydenstricker, whose thoughts constantly yearned toward her native America, gave her daughter many insights into her life as a girl in West Virginia, a life completely at variance with the one with which Pearl was then acquainted. Mrs. Sydenstricker told her daughter of the American Civil War and of the involvement of her family in this catastrophe. She spoke often of her relatives and of the family ancestors. She sang songs and recited poems for the amusement of her children, and she attempted to give them a love of nature and the outdoors. Unforgettable, too, were the Christmas preparations and the sharing of the wondrous delights of the Montgomery Ward catalogues.

There were stories and views of other countries as well. The family doctor was an Indian, and both he and his wife were proficient in speaking English. The young Pearl plied the doctor and his wife with constant questions about their childhoods, their schooling, and about life in India in general. She thus early became aware of the charm and fascination of that country.

She also became friendly with a Japanese lady who lived close at hand and whom she often visited. This lady was well acquainted with people from Burma, Siam, Indonesia, and other nearby countries. Although these individuals lived in China, they were delighted to talk about their native countries, and they furnished a wealth of story and experience. These friendships and experiences not only helped to develop the mind and imagination of an alert, intelligent child but later provided a considerable amount of material for novels and short stories.

Even as a child Pearl Sydenstricker determined to become a writer of stories: "One longs to make what one loves, and above all I loved to hear stories about people. I was a nuisance of a child, I fear, always curious to know about people and why they were as I found them."[8] Since her childhood she has felt a compulsion to write fiction. She has admitted an obsession in this regard and acknowledges that she could never be happy unless she could keep writing.

In addition to listening to stories of various people and places, the growing girl read incessantly. She purchased books with any money she received. Very few children's books were available in China; consequently, much of her reading was in the genre of the novel. These works were principally English novels, since American books were scarce. Her parents did, however, have copies of *Tom Sawyer* and *Huckleberry Finn*, and she read these. But most of her youthful reading was in writers found in the solemn old-fashioned sets of complete or semicomplete works: Shakespeare, Sir Walter Scott, Thackeray, George Eliot, and, above all, Dickens. She began to read *Oliver Twist* when she was seven, and she recalls reading the complete set of Dickens's novels at least once a year over a period of about ten years.[9] Dickens delighted and intrigued her, and later she was to write an enthusiastic essay acknowledging his appeal and his imaginative powers.[10]

Pearl Sydenstricker spoke Chinese before she spoke English, but she came to read and write English sooner than Chinese. She received considerable instruction in English from her mother; Mrs. Sydenstricker insisted on frequent writing exercises, which she discussed and reviewed; and she emphasized the importance of correct English usage. Several of Pearl's youthful writing exercises were published over a period of years in the children's section of the *Shanghai Mercury*, an English-language newspaper. These contributions were signed simply "Novice." Mrs. Sydenstricker encouraged her daughter continually to express her ideas in writing, and this persistent drilling in fundamentals unquestionably proved to be invaluable in developing a feeling for words and an ability to express ideas in a clear, pointed manner.

In addition to the training received in English, the young girl was instructed by Mr. Kung, a Chinese tutor trained in Confucian scholarship, who taught her not only Chinese reading and writing but also many of the principles and tenets of Confucianism. With him she studied Chinese history and became alert to Western imperialism and exploitation in the Far East. She vividly remembers his discussion of the Boxer Rebellion (which, among other things, had earlier forced her, her mother, and her sister to flee to the seacoast). Mr. Kung predicted that his young protegée and all white people would in the future have to flee from China itself in order to save their lives. This consequence would be the result, he maintained, of Western exploitation and injustice.

After the death of the studious Mr. Kung in 1905, Pearl received further education at a mission school and then was sent to board at

Miss Jewell's School in Shanghai. The most valuable part of her year at Miss Jewell's from a literary point of view was undoubtedly her experience in various social works performed by the headmistress.

First, there were visits to an institution for slave girls who had fled the cruel treatment of their owners. Since Pearl could speak Chinese fluently, she carried on long conversations with these unfortunates and learned of their backgrounds and experiences. In an attempt to increase and strengthen Pearl's religious feelings and to show her the necessity of good works, Miss Jewell also took her frequently to an institution that sheltered impoverished and abandoned white women, many of them prostitutes. At this home the teen-age Pearl taught sewing, read books and stories to the inmates, and performed other charitable works. When, however, she went to visit her parents for the spring holidays and told about her participation in Miss Jewell's charitable deeds, her mother refused to permit her return. While her year at Miss Jewell's may not have appreciably increased her book learning, it did broaden and deepen her human experiences and gave her added knowledge of the world.[11] It is notable that artist Victor Beals, who also attended Miss Jewell's School at that time, later recorded how, unlike himself, Pearl had mixed with the people and become familiar with their language and customs. This firsthand acquaintanceship should always be underscored.[12]

That Pearl Sydenstricker's wide background and varied educational training proved beneficial was demonstrated when she came to the United States at the age of seventeen to enter Randolph-Macon Woman's College. There she wrote stories for the college monthly and other campus publications, collaborated on a class play, and won two literary prizes in her senior year. One of these was for the best short story written by a Randolph-Macon student, the other for the best poem.

In college she immediately was conscious of her Chinese background when fellow students regarded her with much curiosity. In order to become part of the group, she realized that she would have to separate to some degree her two worlds; so she began to dress and speak in a more Western manner. By the end of her first year her kinship with an almost new world was complete. She records, however, that she was not fully at ease during her Randolph-Macon years, but she eventually became president of her class and achieved Phi Beta Kappa membership.[13]

More difficult was her adjustment to her parents' relatives, whom she often visited during holidays. She became quite fond of the

Allegheny Mountain area where they lived, but her education and childhood in the Far East prevented her from becoming an integral part of their lives. Nevertheless, while she felt at times that the Eastern and Western strains in her background were divided, she came to realize that these strains were always held together within her mind and heart.

After receiving her degree from Randolph-Macon Woman's College in 1914, she was invited to remain at the school as a teaching assistant in the department of psychology and philosophy. For a time she accepted this position, but the serious illness of her mother recalled her to China before the end of 1914. Of seven children who had been born to Absalom and Caroline Sydenstricker, only three of them lived to adulthood. Pearl's brother, who was ten years older than she, had gone to school in the United States where he had settled permanently. Since the only other surviving child, Grace, was seven years younger than Pearl and since Absalom had to be about his missionary activities, it was most necessary for Pearl to return to tend her mother. She undertook the care of her mother, and she also taught English to senior high school students. In her spare moments she studied written Chinese more intensely. She also replaced her mother as moderator of counseling meetings at which Chinese women discussed their problems and viewpoints. Eventually, Mrs. Sydenstricker regained her health, and her daughter could then devote full time to study and teaching.

Three years after Pearl's return to China she married John Lossing Buck, an American agricultural expert who originally came from Upstate New York. John Lossing Buck was employed by the Presbyterian Mission Board to teach American farming methods to the Chinese. Pearl and her husband went to live in Nanhsüchou in the Anhwei province in North China. There she became intimately acquainted with the ways of the Chinese peasant, his farming methods, his struggles with drought and famine, and the ordinary day-to-day activities of his existence. She accompanied her husband on frequent trips about the countryside; and, while he discussed agricultural methods and techniques with the men, she conversed with the women and children and observed their life. In this area of North China few white people lived, and she was the first white person most of its inhabitants had ever seen. She enjoyed visiting these people, engaging them in long conversations, and learning about their lives. She became fascinated with the farming families that worked incredibly hard and usually made very little money.

Since her husband had a wide knowledge of agricultural matters, she could receive firsthand and accurate knowledge both from her own observation and from his studies. For Pearl Buck these farming people of North China "were the most real, the closest to the earth, to birth and death, to laughter and to weeping. To visit the farm families became my own search for reality, and among them I found the human being as he most nearly is."[14] From this time on there deepened in her a pervading and abiding love of the Chinese peasant, a love which infused her whole being and carried over into her literary works.

After a five-year stay in North China, Pearl Buck and her husband moved southward to Nanking. There John Lossing Buck obtained a professorial position at the University of Nanking as a teacher of agricultural methods, while Pearl accepted a post to teach English literature. This was the beginning of a period of almost ten years during which Pearl Buck taught not only at the University of Nanking, but also at Southeastern University and at Chung Yang University.

In October, 1921, Caroline Sydenstricker, Pearl's mother, died. After her death, her daughter began to write a biography of this missionary wife; it was to be a written memorial for her family. The manuscript was completed and then put away for many years. This biography was actually Pearl Buck's first book, although it was later developed and revised and not published until 1936.

Pearl Buck's life in Nanking was completely different from the rural life of North China. Modern ideas coming from the West were already beginning to infiltrate the old traditional Chinese customs and ways, and many of the young Chinese were in ferment and rebellion. The university students in particular were confused and bewildered. They were reared in a conservative and patriarchal family system which was smug and complacent. Now they faced new liberal ideas and modes of thought. Political and social revolution was in the air, and Bolshevism proclaimed its attractions. These students felt trapped between the old way of life and the new dynamic thoughts of progress. Many of them looked to Western countries for enlightenment; yet they saw inconsistencies and corruption and noticed that Western idealism was frequently at variance with Western practice.[15]

It was a fascinating time to live in China; and, spurred by the writing of her mother's biography, Pearl Buck decided to record some of her impressions of a country caught in the throes of change.

Her first essay on this subject was sent to the *Atlantic Monthly*, which published her article in its January, 1923, issue. Called "In China, Too," this treatise discusses some of the new practices: the popularity of cigarettes, the growing social fraternization of the sexes, American dancing, and the rebellion against parental authority. The marriage problem was very perplexing during these years. In former times parents had chosen the marriage partners and arranged the wedding; now many of the young Chinese were demanding the right to make their own decisions in the Western fashion.

Pearl Buck continued to write about contemporary themes, and additional articles by her began to appear in *Forum*, *The Nation*, and in other magazines. During this time, too, she began to write short stories and to plan her first novel. She, of course, kept reading widely not only the traditional Chinese literature but also Western authors such as Zola, Proust, Thoreau, Hemingway, and, especially, Theodore Dreiser. She particularly admired Dreiser's work and records that, before she was twenty years of age, Dickens was her favorite author; but after twenty, Dreiser became her number one choice, followed by Sinclair Lewis.[16] She was very much interested in character revelation and had high regard for Dreiser, Lewis, and Ellen Glasgow because of their ability to analyze the American character.[17] Many years later, while speaking at a National Education Association convention in New York City, Buck scored the unforgivable neglect of the writings of Dreiser by critics and by the American reading public. In this address she maintained that no other American writer up to that time (1938) could equal the total corpus of his work.[18]

In addition to writing and reading extensively during this period, she pursued an energetic and many-sided career.[19] Unceasing industry and versatility were to become basic characteristics of her life. She kept her position as a university lecturer in literature, performed her household duties, and worried more over the physical condition of Carol, her first child, who showed alarming signs of possible mental retardation. In 1925 she brought this child to the United States for medical treatment; however, she discovered that her little girl would always be mentally handicapped.[20]

To distract herself, she enrolled at Cornell University and studied for her master's degree in the field of English literature. Her husband was also studying there on a year's leave of absence. The following year she received her degree after completing her dissertation, which dealt with the British essayists of the nineteenth century. While at Cornell, since she was desperately in need of money, she decided to compete for the largest prize the university offered, two hundred dollars, which was awarded for the best essay on a topic of international import. Her professorial mentor tried to discourage her from trying for the award because he noted that it was generally given to some student in the history department. Nevertheless, she entered the contest and won the award, the Laura Messenger Prize in history. Her topic was "China and the West," and again the two worlds of East and West met significantly in her life.

II   East Wind: West Wind

In 1925 Pearl Buck wrote a short story which was published in *Asia* magazine under the title "A Chinese Woman Speaks." After this story appeared, she received an unsolicited offer from an American publisher to issue this story provided it was enlarged into a full-length novel. Buck wrote another short story as a sequel to the first narrative, but she felt the framework of "A Chinese Woman Speaks" was too slight and delicate to bear further narrative development. She suggested that the two short stories could perhaps be issued in one volume, but the publishers refused to accept this arrangement.

For some time the two narratives reposed untouched in a drawer, and then she decided to try to interest other publishers in a possible book. She contacted two literary agencies, but they refused to handle story material about China since they maintained that American publishers had very little interest in this area. Eventually, a third literary agent did accept Buck's manuscript but acknowledged that a readers' prejudice existed against Chinese subject matter. In time, however, this agency discovered a publisher.

Pearl Buck had circulated the two short stories under the title *Winds of Heaven*. Since the publishers did not favor that heading, the subtitle of the manuscript, *East Wind: West Wind*, was used. The publishers were also distressed by the large number of clichés and hackneyed phrases used in the text. Buck had deliberately included such expressions from books she had read in English because in Chinese literature it is considered a mark of fine style to use well-known diction and phraseology found in the works of great writers. When she revised her manuscript she omitted the borrowed phrases and put the ideas in her own style. After the revised text was submitted, the book was accepted for publication. On April 10, 1930, *East Wind: West Wind* was issued, the first of Pearl Buck's many books of fiction.

East Wind: West Wind, which was popular enough to go through three printings in less than a year, concerns a young Chinese married couple, a girl named Kwei-lan and her husband, who is a physician. Following the old Chinese custom, Kwei-lan's family had betrothed her to her future husband even before she was born. Kwei-lan and her family believe in the ancient traditions and ways, but her husband, who has been educated abroad for twelve years, believes in equality and in the modern trends and democratic practices of the West. From this division of allegiance comes the basic conflict of the story. This conflict was a vital problem in twentieth-century China and was especially perplexing in the 1920s and 1930s.

Kwei-lan writes her story in the form of a long epistolary monologue to a woman friend who came from a foreign land but who has lived in China. Kwei-lan chooses this unnamed woman as a listener because the woman knows both the ways of the West and the practices of the East. The narrative is initiated because Kwei-lan is at first unhappy in her marriage and she needs to relate her unfortunate plight to a sympathetic ear.

On her bridal night Kwei-lan's husband told her that he regarded her as an equal, as a companion, and not as a slave or as a piece of property. He explained that he wanted to follow the new modes of Western life, and he agreed to give her time to adjust to this situation. Kwei-lan is astounded, for in the ancient manner, she regards herself as a mere subordinate to her husband, and she cannot understand his wishes. She is further bewildered when her husband refuses to allow her to perform the standard duties and services to his mother. Although it was customary for a married couple to live with the husband's parents, Kwei-lan's husband insists that he and his wife live in a Western-style house. When Kwei-lan meets some of her husband's Occidental friends, she appears uncomfortable, finds Western ways strange, and worries about the aloofness of her spouse who absorbs himself completely in his medical interests. Although his family is extremely wealthy, and he could choose to live a life of idleness and ease, he does not wish to do so. He develops an active practice as a doctor.

Her husband becomes very insistent that she unbind her feet. This custom of tightly wrapping a young girl's foot in cloth so that her feet will be small and dainty and her walk very graceful was one of the most ancient and widely practiced Chinese customs. But Kwei-lan's physician husband realizes that it is an unhealthy practice that leads to broken bones and deformed limbs. Kwei-lan is shocked by her husband's suggestion: she has always regarded dainty feet as an important feature of beauty. When she was younger and had suffered the continual soaking in warm water and the tight bandaging, she had been consoled by her mother's conviction that her future husband would admire the beauty of her tiny feet. She now learns that her husband is vehemently opposed to this practice.

Kwei-lan carries this problem to her own mother, who is astounded by her daughter's story. Although she has reared Kwei-lan properly in the old ways, her mother informs her that she must obey her husband. Kwei-lan is told that, because she has married, she is no longer a member of her parents' family; she belongs now to her husband. Gradually, because of the affection she has toward her husband and because of her slowly advancing knowledge of the new ways, Kwei-lan unbinds her feet and makes other concessions to her husband's desires. When he understands that she is willing to try to follow Western customs, Kwei-lan's husband ceases to be aloof, begins to teach her some basic science, and educates her in modern ideas.[21] Kwei-lan is delighted with her husband's attention and interest, and her marriage is now successful.

Part Two of *East Wind: West Wind*, a separate story, concerns Kwei-lan's brother, and it adds the problem of interracial marriage to the basic conflict between the ways of the East and those of the West. Again Kwei-lan narrates the events and again writes to the same correspondent.

In the first part of the book we knew only that Kwei-lan's mother and father were upset when her brother refused to marry the girl to whom his family had betrothed him. He then traveled overseas to study science. Now we learn that he wishes to marry an American girl, called only Mary in the story. He writes to his parents for permission to marry her and to break his childhood betrothal to the daughter of Li. His parents refuse to grant his request; they order him to return and to perform his proper family duty. However, he weds Mary in the United States and returns to China with her.

His parents are furious. At first his mother refuses to receive the foreign wife, and his father absents himself on business. Eventually, Kwei-lan's brother dresses his wife in Chinese garb and manages to present her, but again the parents will not accept this relationship. Kwei-lan's attempts at mediation are abortive. The mother becomes further distraught and eventually ill. Under this circumstance, she writes to her son and agrees to have him and his wife come to live in one of the courts of the family home. When this is accomplished, the wife is ostracized by the family and forced to live a more or less cloistered existence. After the mother learns that the foreign wife is pregnant, she sinks into an even more depressed and debilitated condition. Soon she dies without having recognized the foreigner as her son's wife. According to Chinese law, unless one of the parents acknowledges the marriage, the son cannot receive his legal inheritance.

After his mother's death the son asks his father for legal recognition of the marriage. The request is refused. The son is again informed that he must marry the daughter of Li and, thereby, uphold the family pledge. In an exceedingly dramatic passage Kwei-lan's brother repudiates his family and insists that his name be removed from the rolls of the clan. He cuts himself off completely from his relatives and ancestors. He and his wife move out of his father's house, he acquires a teaching position in a local government school, and his wife delivers a son.

Kwei-lan relates the distress surrounding the birth of this child. His mother has been separated from her country and her people, and his father has broken ancestral ties. Yet, at the same time, the child has brought about a union of the old and new, of the East and the West. She concludes that the newly born child will come to understand both worlds and become much stronger and wiser on that account.

East Wind: West Wind is usually spoken of as a novel, but, in fact, it consists of two definite short stories with a decided break between them. The first narrative is more poetic and romantic; the second, more sparse and moralistic. The Dreiser influence, which we are to see displayed particularly in *The Good Earth*, is nonexistent in this book.

East Wind: West Wind is written in a much more delicately wrought and self-conscious style than is found in the later works of Pearl Buck. While basically simple in form, the mode of expression is somewhat artificial. The style tends to be choppy, slow-paced, heavily romantic, often strikingly exotic, reminiscent in many of its colorful images of Edward Fitzgerald's translation of *The Rubaiyat of Omar Khayyam*. The prose is often too consciously flowery, and several "purple passages" also appear too obviously calculated for effect. The framework of having Kwei-lan write the details of the story to the foreign lady who has lived in China becomes increasingly artificial, forced, and wearisome as the narrative progresses.

A certain amount of extraneous description occurs, for example, some rather unnecessarily detailed portraits of the concubines in Kwei-lan's father's house. Such descriptions are yanked into the narrative evidently for background and coloring, but the majority of the descriptions serve the useful purpose of enumerating the manners of aristocratic Chinese families and of underscoring the complete differences in customs between China and the West. Here the book is most successful. Both the situation and the reality of the problem present themselves in a credible fashion, and the author manages to convey a definite flavor of setting, scene, and authenticity of locale— later a basic characteristic of Pearl Buck's fiction.

At times sentimentalism predominates, particularly in Kwei-lan's feeling for her family home, in her joy over the birth of a son, and in her reaction to her brother's child. There is, also, a tendency to dwell too long on the similarity of Kwei-lan's and her sister-in-law's reaction to the beauty and winningness of babies, although, of course, this reinforces the one-world point of view. Perhaps Buck overlabors the point that, in their basic emotions and feelings people the world over, regardless of race, are much alike.

In spite of its deficiencies, *East Wind: West Wind* contains several effective passages, and the theme is meaningful. The characters are caught in a modern dilemma, and the happy resolution in Kwei-lan's case and the semitragic resolution in her brother's are convincingly rendered. The objections of the Chinese mother and father to a foreign daughter-in-law strike a common chord, and the tensions produced from their prejudices and instinctive attitudes bring focus to the problem. Truth is at the core of *East Wind: West Wind*, but at times the veneer of romanticism and sentimentalism blurs and softens this truth.

In an overall view, *East Wind: West Wind* remains more interesting for its promise than for its effectiveness as a book in its own right. Although it reveals several weaknesses—uncertainty in handling a story framework, tendencies to stylistic artificiality, and a pronounced sentimentality—it points up the fact that Buck has a thorough knowledge of her subject and possesses a fundamental narrative sense. Her first book of fiction also demonstrates that she is a novelist who is in the happy position of understanding both sides in various conflicts between two different worlds, and between the old and new customs. She has found a solid hook on which she can hang innumerable stories revolving around these themes.

Perhaps the most important aspect of *East Wind: West Wind* was that it gave Pearl Buck the necessary confidence to continue in the field of fiction since she now realized that a market for stories using Chinese materials was available. That this knowledge was vital to her, she has herself noted, since at that time the only thing she knew well enough to write about was China.[22]

Before *East Wind: West Wind* was published in 1930, Pearl Buck had completed a novel; however, before it could be sent to a publisher for consideration, the Nationalist-Communist uprising in 1926–27 caused much havoc and destruction. When the soldiers entered Buck's home in Nanking, the manuscript of this novel was completely destroyed. She never attempted to rewrite it, and no trace of the original exists. Up to this point then, Pearl Buck had written three books—the first draft of the biography of her mother, *East Wind: West Wind*, and the novel destroyed during the revolutionary army uprising—as well as several articles and short stories. This apprenticeship and background in the field of writing and literature not only give a good idea of the experience Pearl Buck had amassed at this time but also quite firmly shatter the misconception, which one still occasionally hears, that *The Good Earth* was written without much literary preparation by a completely inexperienced author.

CHAPTER 2

The Good Earth

THE publication of *The Good Earth* on March 2, 1931, in Buck's fortieth year proved to be a literary phenomenon. This lengthy narrative, covering many years in the history and life of a Chinese peasant family, became one of the most famous best sellers in the history of American fiction and achieved wide popularity abroad. This novel was translated into more than thirty different languages, not including the many pirated editions.[1] At least seven different translations of the novel were made into the Chinese language alone.[2] This saga won the Pulitzer Prize, was instrumental in winning for its author the Howells Medal for Distinguished Fiction a few years later, and became an important factor in her being awarded the Nobel Prize. *The Good Earth* was also converted into a Broadway play[3] and into a memorable motion picture with unforgettable performances by Paul Muni and Luise Rainer.[4]

From her life in China Pearl Buck had conceived a warm admiration for the ordinary people of the land.[5] China was an agricultural country, and these farming folk comprised four-fifths of the total population. Despite their overwhelming numbers, these peasants were the most abused group in the country; they were continually mistreated by governmental officials, bandits, and landlords. In addition, they had to struggle to exist against the terrible perils of flood and famine. Even when they were forced to flee southward or to other areas because of such catastrophes, they returned to the land whenever possible. Buck was convinced that these good, solid farmers formed the heart of China.[6] Her interest in them as people gave her a starting point, and love and affirmation for the Chinese peasant became one of the principal ingredients of her thought and writing.

When Pearl Buck sat down to write the novel that proved to be her greatest book, she felt that she had the experience to write a meaningful work. She could recall vividly the North China scene where she had lived for five years and she could remember that Nanking, a site with which she was particularly well acquainted, often received farm refugees from the north. The impetus for her book was the anger she had felt because the common people of China were so often oppressed and abused.

When she was prepared to write *The Good Earth*, she acknowledges that "there was no plot or plan. Only the man and the woman and their children stood there before me."[7] Later, she came to realize, however, that these people were not just Chinese; they were representative of farming people the world over. They were universal in their struggles, in their joys, in their disappointments. This quality was immediately recognized by readers of the novel.

The Good Earth had its literary genesis in a story called "The Revolutionist," published in the September, 1928, issue of *Asia* magazine.[8] The chief character in this narrative was named Wang Lung. When she began writing *The Good Earth*, Pearl Buck used Wang Lung as the basis for her principal male character. During the composition of the book she intended the novel to be called "Wang Lung"; however, the title was changed after the completed manuscript reached the publisher.

"The Revolutionist" is a slight, seriocomic narrative about an impoverished Chinese farmer. On his frequent trips to Nanking he meets and hears the speeches of revolutionists. Musing on how he will look when the poor people become rich, Wang Lung decides to have his head shaved. Since only the revolutionists cut off their hair, he acquires the title of "Wang the Revolutionist." Seven of the rebels are caught and beheaded; and Wang, who is innocent of any sedition, fears for his life. When the revolution occurs some time later, Wang participates in the looting and manages to collect a little money and a few incidentals, but his lot has not improved.

"The Revolutionist" bears only two rather negligible resemblances to *The Good Earth*. In the novel Wang Lung does hear some of the preaching of the revolutionists, and he does participate in mob looting. The similarities, however, are slight and inconsequential. In *The Good Earth* both similarities are handled with much more finesse and elaboration than the short story would permit. Further, the novel considerably elevates the character of Wang: he is no longer a somewhat idle and completely naïve fool; he is no longer a comic figure. His character takes on seriousness; he receives dimension and a satisfying solidity, and becomes vivid to the reader.

This vividness of both character and scene, which is not found in

"The Revolutionist," distinguishes *The Good Earth*. Even when the novel has not been read for some time, one recalls Wang's apprehension over his approaching wedding, the suffering induced by famine and flood, O-lan's industry and stoicism, Wang's choice of a concubine when he becomes wealthy and restless, and his sons' almost indecently eager desire to sell the land as soon as their father passes away.

Part of the reason for this vividness rests in the universality of the novel's various portraits. Not only does the particularity of the wedding day loom on a general level of credibility, but several other events ring true, surpassing mere time and locale: the expectation and joy over the birth of the first child, the suffering induced by poverty and sickness, the malice of some relatives, the tragedy of death in a family, the father's pride in his educated sons, the ingratitude of children to parents, the jealousy and quarreling of brothers, the difficulties caused by war and the catastrophes of nature. These and numerous other happenings convey, as one critic remarks, the "continuity of human experience" and render "into universal terms immemorial human attitudes."[9] It is just this similarity to truth and to our own individual lives that makes *The Good Earth* stir deep patterns of recognition within the minds and hearts of its readers. It portrays life as it is: all true, all believable. *The Good Earth* is one of those novels that particularly supports the logic of E. M. Forster's memorable remark, "The final test of a novel will be our affection for it."

Portrayed, too, with graphic authority is the ebb and flow of life, its change and perpetual movements, not only seasonally from spring to winter, from seed planting to harvest, but also a cycle of both family and humanity. Past links with present and present links with future. In presenting an American Academy of Arts and Letters gold medal for fiction to Thornton Wilder, Buck said of this author: "Part of his youth was spent in China, and no one can live in that tremendous country, where time is measured in centuries and space by landscapes as various as the world provides, without being shaped by eternities."[10] This same sense of "being shaped by eternities" is one of the characteristics of *The Good Earth*.

As a *roman-fleuve*, *The Good Earth* carries us through several generations of the Wang clan and analyzes the growth of the family as it develops in power and wealth. Such families in China, Buck has declared, begin on the land: and, if favorable circumstances present themselves, the family increases in stature and importance. But, she insists, such families develop from their land roots; they grow from the soil.

The cyclic movement emphasized in the development of the Wang family is counterpoised by the decline of the House of Hwang. When Wang Lung came originally to the House of Hwang to receive his bride, he was overwhelmed by the beauty and grandeur of the magnificent Hwang estate. At this time Wang was a poor, timid, and embarrassed farmer; and his future wife was a mere slave in the Hwang kitchen. Wang cowered as the satin-robed Old Mistress of the family sat on a splendidly carved dais and presented him with O-lan. Eventually, however, with the passing of years, the House of Hwang, through extravagance, corruption, and poor management, falls into decline. Many of the outer courts of the Hwang estate come to be occupied by impoverished squatters from the city streets; the beautiful halls fall into disrepair, and several of the buildings waste into ruin. After the passing of many years Wang Lung is able to purchase this decaying mansion for the use of his own family. This contrast of rise and fall is not heavily underscored; however, it does furnish a quiet but grim strain to the movement of time.

Another notable aspect giving *The Good Earth* much of its appeal and penetration is its ability to present universality even though it deals with a race with which people in English-speaking countries are not especially familiar except, of course, in Fu Manchu distortions and similar fanciful exaggerations. James Gray declares that Buck has enabled the Western reader to know China with "sanity, compassion and understanding,"[11] and another critic maintains that *The Good Earth* made "American readers aware, in the lives of a completely alien people, of universal human bonds."[12] Carl Van Doren asserts that in "the United States, which had a special friendly liking for China, *The Good Earth* for the first time made the Chinese seem as familiar as neighbors. Pearl Buck," he continues, "had added to American fiction one of its larger provinces."[13] This accomplishment is achieved through vividness of character portrayal, authenticity of setting, and the universality in reaction to birth, marriage, suffering, death, and other basic, vital occurrences.

In addition, careful handling and emphasis on both the precise and the appropriate descriptive details further enhance the similarities of experience. The reader is furnished with excellent descriptions of such things as New Year's customs, marriage ceremonies, burial rituals, meal preparations, and soil cultivation. The descriptions are never overdrawn or excessive; their conciseness always centers on concrete, closely observed, "essential" details; and, although the scene which we behold is unfolding in a distant land and many of the practices and traditions are exotic or picturesque, we see the essential logic and reality of these customs in their time and place. In its economy and in its laconic but vital lyricism, the descriptive passages in *The Good Earth* often remind us of Ernest Hemingway's writing. The style bears no dross; only descriptive details necessary to convey the scene or to reinforce the mood are recorded.[14]

The style of *The Good Earth* is one of the novel's most impressive characteristics. This style is based on the manner of the old Chinese narrative sagas related and written down by storytellers and on the mellifluous prose of the King James version of the Bible. At certain times Buck declared that her style was Chinese rather than biblical.[15] She explained that she learned to speak Chinese and used Chinese idioms. Therefore, when she wrote about Chinese subject matter, the narrative formed itself mentally into the Chinese language, and she then translated this material into English. She asserted that her prose was based on idiomatic Chinese and that she was often uncertain about the English qualities of the style.[16] At other times she admitted, however, the combined influences of the old Chinese sagas and the King James version.[17] Many similarities exist between the two forms, ranging from the use of parallelism to an old-fashioned, even archaic, form of expression. The King James version of the Bible was often studied and read aloud in Pearl Buck's childhood home, and much of its phraseology remained in the young girl's mind, both consciously and subconsciously, and became a part of her stylistic forms and patterns. This double influence of the Chinese saga and the Bible, then, explains most accurately her stylistic mannerisms.

Pearl Buck's writing in *The Good Earth* is characterized by simplicity, concreteness, a stress on long serpentine sentences, parallelism, balance, and repetition of words. Although the majority of the sentences are lengthy, they break into shorter, sometimes choppy, segments of thought which undulate in movement. The style, generally slow-paced, evinces a quiet stateliness and seriousness. It does not at all rival the color or richness of the biblical imagery, principally because it follows the simplicity of word choice of the Chinese saga rather than the more imaginative and exotic coloring of the Old and New Testaments. At certain times Buck's style achieves poetical suggestion, but never is the imbalance between the normal and the more poetic so pronounced as to produce isolated "purple passages," as was the case in *East Wind: West Wind.*

The style of *The Good Earth* is unusually appropriate for the saga-like story. The simplicity and the slow but steady movement of the prose fit harmoniously the heroic quality of the narrative. Carl Van Doren spoke with understanding when he categorized the style of the novel and its relationship to its material in the following manner:

Fluent and flexible, it was simple in idiom and cadence, like a realistic pastoral or a humane saga.... In *The Good Earth* ... the style is regularly supported by the matter. The style gives an agreeable music to the convincing history. Nor was it more convincing in America, in the midst of the depression, than elsewhere. The depression touched all peoples. Even where they were not threatened with immediate famine, as in the starvation chapters of the book, they saw that complex systems of life had broken down. It was not certain that anything but the land remained. Wang's hunger for land, and his obstinate clinging to it once he had it, touched responsive sentiments in every country.[18]

Discussing the clarity of Buck's prose and observing that her style seems completely appropriate to her characters in time and place, Phyllis Bentley asserts that

Pearl Buck never uses a Chinese word, never needs to explain one. Even "Mah-Jongg," for example, is called "sparrow dominoes"—and very rigidly, since that is what the Chinese word means to the Chinese. On the other hand, Mrs. Buck never, I think, uses a word for which a literal translation into Chinese could not be found. The effect of her prose is to translate what the Chinese mean into language which means that to us ... [Her prose is] grave, quiet, biblical speech, full of dignity, in which Mrs. Buck, without ever "raising her voice," is able to render both the deepest and the lightest emotions.[19]

Biblical style is a feature of the modern saga, and Alexander Cowie points out that *The Good Earth* is closely allied to the epic or saga. He calls Pearl Buck's best book the most popular American novel written in this vein. Noting the objectivity and rather stoical approach toward their material of the writers of the saga narrative, he records Buck's affinity to the work of Ole Rölvaag.[20] He observes further that although such saga-like stories avoid subjectivity and moralizing, they contain a strong strain of sympathy toward the characters and scenes pictured.[21] This quality is very marked in *The Good Earth*.

In structure, *The Good Earth* uses a chronological form which proceeds at a fairly regular pace. Some climaxes occur, although they do not reach too much higher than the normal incidents in the story. The movement is slower and somewhat less arresting after O-lan's death, but some slackening is inevitable in a *roman-fleuve*. Phyllis Bentley's comments on Buck's structure are fitting:

[Her] stories take the epic rather than the dramatic form; that is to say, they are chronological narratives of a piece of life, seen from one point of view, straightforward, without devices; they have no complex plots, formed of many strands skillfully twisted, but belong to the single-strand type, with the family, however, rather than the individual as a unit.[22]

Although *The Good Earth* places much emphasis on the family unit, and the analysis of the family fortunes is pivotal, the main characters are studied in detail. The portrayal of Wang Lung's character is starkly frank. His strengths and weaknesses are candidly examined and bared before the reader; and while, on the basis of a superficial reading, he might appear to be a one-dimensional figure, he runs the whole gamut of human emotions. He can be gauche and timid, as on the first visit to the House of Hwang to claim his bride; he can be stubborn and resolute, as in his determination to buy more land; he can be servile and pusillanimous when he learns that his uncle is a member of the robber band; he can be tender and gentle to his mentally retarded daughter and to his child concubine Pear Blossom; he can be a complete fool in the hands of certain women, as in his first overwhelming passion for Lotus; he can be incredibly inconsiderate and unfeeling as when he deprives O-lan of her two cherished pearls; he can be snobbish and hard-hearted in his attitude toward the squatters in the outer courtyards of the House of Hwang; he can be crafty and calculating in his gift of opium to his uncle and the latter's wife; he can be idle and restless; he can be dedicated and industrious; he can in his old age seek only comfort and quiet, and humor his sons too much. In these and in other ways he becomes a complex and many-sided figure; and, although he is dominated by a ruling passion for the land, he is above all a human being with all the whims, emotions, quirks, inconsistencies, contradictions, and variable attitudes that go to make up a living individual.

Equally striking is the character of O-lan. Her indefatigability and her almost interminable silences are constantly impressed on the reader's mind. And yet she, too, has certain quite understandable notions. She wants her first son to be dressed in finery, and she must make special cakes so that she can return to the House of Hwang during the New Year's festivities and show how well she has fared, what a good marriage she has made, and how healthy and handsome her first-born looks. This pride is particularly touching because O-lan wants and expects so little from life. O-lan also shows understandable humanity when she protests the presence of Lotus's serving woman in her house. This serving woman was O-lan's superior in the House of Hwang and was exceptionally cruel and critical. But even O-lan's protestations cannot move Wang Lung to remedy this situation. Nevertheless, O-lan can at least use passive resistance, and this she does in her own inimitable fashion. O-lan has few pleasures; yet her last wish before her death is to see her eldest son married so that a grandson may be conceived for her husband and a great-grandson for her father-in-law. When the marriage has been accomplished, she can die happily with the consolation that, although she has been a slave, she herself has produced sons and there will be children for the future. In his critique of *The Good Earth* Oscar Cargill emphasizes O-lan's devotion to her husband under all conditions and concludes with a fitting epitaph: "Earth of the earth-earthy, she triumphs in the end over her rivals, though her ugliness goes clear to the bone."[23]

As might be expected, the other figures in the novel are not so well realized as Wang Lung and O-lan. It is true that Wang's father is a lifelike portrait and one remembers his cough (the first sound his son heard in the morning), his delight in his grandsons, and his general somnolence. The sons of Wang Lung are, however, rather sketchily drawn. They tend to be types: the eldest, extravagant and concerned with propriety; the second son, grasping and tight-fisted; the youngest, rebellious and undisciplined. Wang's uncle, too, is a type whose connection with the robbers seems somewhat improbable. He also appears to yield too passively to the possibility of an opium stupor. One suspects that the uncle is too consciously manipulated by the author in order to free Wang Lung from trouble with the robbers and, further, that the uncle is given opium—as a deus ex machina—to remove him from the scene as expeditiously as possible.

Some improbability appears in Wang Lung's rather timid and careless yielding to the grandiose plans of his eldest son to restore the grandeur of the Hwang home. Wang is too passive at these moments, too easily swayed by his son. In general, however, it is difficult to disagree with Oscar Cargill's belief that the book's greatest merit "is the conviction it carries of verisimilitude to all the vicissitudes of Chinese life—nothing changes or passes which does not seem probable."[24]

Mention should be made of the haze of romanticism that hovers over and about the novel. Buck has wisely avoided the artificial romanticism and the obvious sentimentalism that marred *East Wind: West Wind.* Yet the story of *The Good Earth,* although it maintains a convincing realism, takes on a certain exotic remoteness which lends additional charm to its episodes. The strange is made familiar, and the familiar is made pleasantly strange. Indeed, certain sections of Wordsworth's preface to the *Lyrical Ballads* apply perfectly here: "The principal object . . . was to choose incidents and situations from common life . . . to throw over them a certain coloring of imagination, whereby ordinary things should be presented to the mind in an unusual aspect; and further, and above all, to make these incidents and situations interesting by tracing in them, truly though not ostentatiously, the primary laws of our nature." The faraway coloring of *The Good Earth* lights the familiar elements with new freshness and appeal. Realism and romanticism blend in just the right proportions. Life is given the glow of legend, and legend is given the aura of life.

The motto opposite the book's first page taken from Proust's *Swann's Way* alludes to the phrase from Vinteuil's sonata which had so affected Swann with truth, love, and deep feelings for humanity. This motto relates that the musician Vinteuil refused to add his own subjective feelings and emotions to the composition. He had captured life and truth in the music, and he did not wish to distort the music with his personal attitudes. This motto thus heralds the objectivity of *The Good Earth.* Buck claims that she is not inventing; she is simply transposing life to paper. William Lyon Phelps once remarked that, if *The Good Earth*'s author were unknown, a reader could not detect whether the writer was male or female, a radical or a conservative, a follower of a religious creed or an atheist.[25] So objective and impersonal is the novel that it almost seems to exist apart from authorial composition.

Other than proclaiming the eternal cycle of birth and death, growth and decay, and continual change, the "message" of *The Good Earth* has to be inferred since it is never explicitly stated. The novel does suggest that diligent toil may achieve some satisfaction but that luxury may corrupt and ruin "the spiritual meaning of life."[26] Certainly, too, *The Good Earth* does champion "the old American belief in hard work, thrift, ceaseless enterprise and the value of living close to the land."[27] But, while such a "message" may be extracted from the book, such a theme is not presented as a didactic preachment. The "message" exists simply as a corollary of the movement of life itself. Even where a moral or lesson can be drawn, for example, in Wang Lung's contempt for the common people, once he himself achieves wealth and position, no exhortation or sermon is attempted. There rings in our mind only universal truth: this is the way life is; the way people are.

Life's successes, failures, passions, devotions, high points of joy, distressing moments of sadness, constant variety and change, in short the great adventure that is life—these aspects of existence pass continually in review. The novel is didactic only in the sense that life can be so. By watching *The Good Earth*'s pageant of living move before us, we come to know not only ourselves more deeply, but life itself more fully and more comprehensively. Perhaps this is one of the strongest reasons why, in the words of Henry Seidel Canby, *The Good Earth* "belongs among the permanent contributions to world literature of our time."[28]

Oscar Cargill has noted some general similarities between Pearl Buck's *House of Earth* trilogy (of which *The Good Earth* is the first part) and the Rougon-Macquart family saga of Émile Zola. Cargill maintains that the Wang family and the Rougon-Macquart clan are both representative of their respective periods and countries; that the Wangs' rise comes from one man's desire for the earth, which contrasts in part to the greed of Madame Felicite Rougon; that there is much emphasis on details of love and birth, family quarrels, etc.; and that Buck and Zola are alike in their hatred of the trader class.[29] He points out the similarity in title between *The Good Earth* and Zola's *La Terre*, but stresses that Buck and Zola are different in temperament—she is unemotional, simple, and disciplined; Zola is moody, excitable, and garrulous. He concludes that the difference between the two is fundamentally a difference in style, not in viewpoint.

Pearl Buck has acknowledged the influence of Zola,[30] and it is almost immediately evident. Certainly *The Good Earth* is Naturalistic in many ways: in its documentary approach to its material, in its detached and objective presentation, in its stress on factors of environment and heredity, in its accuracy of setting and descriptive details, and in its interest in impoverished and earthy people who dwell on the lower strata of social class. Yet, at the same time, several differences exist between Buck's approach and Zola's. She is much less interested in sordidness, brutality, and squalor; and her emphasis on these factors arises out of a more balanced and wholesome interest in things as they are than from a deliberate emphasis on the seamier aspects of life in order to shock and horrify.[31]

In commenting on the charge that the character of Wang Lung is coarse, Buck retorted that her protagonist must be viewed in the time and place in which he lived. On the basis of modern drawing-room society, Wang Lung may appear coarse. Yet, Buck maintained, Wang Lung must be portrayed as he is; he must be true to life.[32] She herself does not regard him as coarse but only as real, normal, and natural in his time and locale.

Pearl Buck's attitudes are not those of a thorough-going Naturalist. The principal difference between Zola's Naturalism and the Naturalistic aspects in *The Good Earth* resides in the authors' attitudes toward free will. In Zola's world, people are oppressed by social and economic forces which overwhelm the human individual and render him almost helpless. Zola's characters are caught in a deterministic world, shaped by heredity and environment. In *The Good Earth*, on the other hand, free will exerts considerable influence. When Wang Lung's uncle and his wife bewail their unfortunate destiny and blame their misfortunes on things that they cannot control, Wang Lung notes that their poverty is basically a question of too much idleness, gossiping, and gambling. These are the reasons for the lack of money and success characteristic of Wang's relatives early in the novel. Wang Lung himself rises above his environmental limitations through hard work, thriftiness, and dedication. It is true that the money acquired during the mass looting serves as the primary lever which puts Wang in a position to gain a solid economic footing, but only through industry and initiative does he rise to affluence. Buck's own philosophy is the opposite of Zola's. In her autobiography she relates that she "learned early that trouble and suffering can always be relieved if there is the will to do it, and in that knowledge I have found escape from despair throughout my life."[33] In another passage she remarks that "man can shape his world if he does not resign himself to ignorance."[34]

For the sake of strict semantic accuracy, Realism rather than Naturalism would be a more accurate term to apply to Pearl Buck's work. The pessimism and despair of a writer like Zola are far removed from Buck's more affirmative approach to things as they exist and from the basic meliorism which her writing in general displays. She stands as an optimist rather than a pessimist, although she often hears and records the "eternal note of sadness." Van Wyck Brooks correctly links *The Good Earth* with the work of Balzac, Molière, and Dickens, writers who convey a positive and sustaining approach toward life.[35]

Buck, however, is fond of using the word Naturalism in connection with her own work. On more than one occasion she speaks of the Naturalism of Chinese life, and by this she means the Chinese frankness in sexual matters, in language, and on occasions of birth and death. The Naturalism of *The Good Earth* is, therefore, simply a recording of the way Chinese life in the farming areas is; there is no attempt to slant or distort the material into a Naturalistic vein, or to shape it consciously to fit a preconceived Naturalistic mode of writing. The Naturalism of this novel is its candid look at life as it exists. Buck admires the naturalness and veracity of the Chinese attitude as opposed to the American Puritanic attitude. She once praised Ernest Hemingway for having the courage to approach life from a Naturalistic point of view. While indicating that Hemingway's Naturalism was something relatively new to Americans, she remarked that such an attitude was extremely common in China. The Naturalism of Chinese life, she explained, is simply truth; and she recalled that even in her early childhood years in China she had witnessed natural events involving men and women that the average American would regard with shock and distaste.[36]

In her early work Buck particularly admired aspects of the Naturalistic writing. She has, as previously noted, expressed considerable respect for the writings of Theodore Dreiser. The close reporting, the concern for economic, social, and environmental factors, the fundamental interest in the basic emotions and problems of life, and the seemingly "objective" approach to material unquestionably related to Buck's own experiences and viewpoints. But she was unwilling to concur with the Naturalistic notion of determinism since she valued too highly the elements of self-reliance and individual initiative which she had found in human nature. The world of *The Good Earth* may be often sad, tragic, defeating, ironic, and frustrating; but it is never a world without hope, never one which would completely debilitate the striving individual. Like Goethe, she approves man's Faustian sense of *streben*. She, too, affirms life and man's aspirations.

CHAPTER 3

Fame That Was Not Fleeting

T HE *Good Earth* succeeded in making Pearl S. Buck's name a household word. Yet the two-edged sword of fame, while it may bring success, wealth, prestige, and publicity, offers, at the same time, a target for attack, criticism, and jealousy. Further, fame makes stringent demands and requirements: it places heavy and steady pressure on its recipients to maintain their place among the elect. In the case of an author who has written a widely acclaimed literary work, the weight of fame can become oppressive. Sinclair Lewis once confessed to Pearl Buck that he frequently wished he had never written *Main Street* since he was weary of people focusing on that novel to the exclusion of his other books.[1] The author whom fame has chosen also faces the problem of trying to live up to a great book, of knowing that every one of his subsequent works will be compared, probably unfavorably, to his former significant achievement. The "one-book" label hangs over the head of many writers and furnishes an additional burden for them to bear. Even when the great "one-book" has been approached or nearly equaled in later writings, it is often difficult to find critics and readers willing to acknowledge such a feat. All of these manifold aspects of literary fame relate to Buck's career after the publication of her best-known novel.

I *Portrait of China Attacked*

After the impact of *The Good Earth*, Pearl Buck's portrayal of Chinese life drew much censure from some Chinese critics who insisted that the picture of Chinese life she presented was untrue. One of the earliest indignant discussions of Buck's work appeared in the *New Republic*, where Younghill Kang attacked *The Good Earth*. He found "The author's picture of excessive child bearing" completely "out of proportion."[2] He asserted that Buck's characters talk without propriety and with "frankness, a thing abhorrent to the traditional

Oriental."[3] Further, he insisted that no man would become sexually involved with his own slave and that, if a father did such a thing, his sons would probably commit suicide because of the disgrace. So enthusiastic and so chauvinistic in his argument did Kang become that he further maintained that no woman in China, not even a slave girl, would have premarital sexual experience.

The preposterous generalizations and the frankly extreme tone of Kang's comments immediately startle the reader and cause him to expect inaccuracy and excessive partisanship. One can more or less negate Kang's remarks on the basis of one's general knowledge of human nature. In addition to the statements quoted above, Kang makes much of what he regards as Pearl Buck's emphasis on romantic love which, he believes, reduces Confucian society "to a laughable pandemonium."[4] In fact, relatively little "romantic" love exists in *The Good Earth*, but the main point to be remembered against Kang's thesis is that Buck is not delineating a strictly "Confucian" society. Younghill Kang is also adamant in his insistence that no peasant could rise from the land as Wang Lung manages to do since, in Kang's view, Chinese "rise, if at all, only by force of manners and scholarship."[5]

What is seen clearly in Kang's critique is the feeling that, since Pearl Buck has given an unflattering portrait of Chinese life, she has presented an untrue picture.[6] Kang's comments exemplify the tendency among many Chinese and Far Eastern intellectuals to judge China and their countries on the basis of the educated and scholarly classes. Kang's attitude is representative of an especially petty, narrow, and unscholarly approach on the part of some members of the intellectual class.

The most vehement attack on Pearl Buck for allegedly giving a false view of Chinese life is found in an article by Professor Kiang Kang-Hu published in the *New York Times*.[7] Kiang, Professor of Chinese Studies at McGill University in Montreal, charged Pearl Buck with exaggerating and distorting certain aspects of Chinese life and with making errors of fact. First of all, Kiang commences with the thesis that non-Chinese writers cannot write accurately of life in China. He maintains that the peasants and the lower-class people about whom Pearl Buck writes are rare in China and that such people are not representative of China and her people. Professor Kiang leads his readers to the inference that there are no bandits in China any more because *Sons* (the sequel to *The Good Earth*), which deals with banditry, is influenced by *Shui Hu Chuan*, a traditional Chinese story of life in the Middle Ages. The inference is that bandits in China went out of fashion after that period so that, if someone wants to write a book about robber bands, he must base his material on ancient stories. Yet such an outrageous suggestion is refuted by news stories, personal experiences, and even histories concerned with twentieth-century China. Kiang says nothing of the bandit groups in *The Good Earth*, but he obviously thinks such episodes unrealistic and exaggerated.

Kiang finds fault with many of Pearl Buck's details. He denies as completely false the notion that any Chinese would send for priests to call a woman's soul back to life after her suicide (an incident described in *East Wind: West Wind*). He insists that no Chinese would drop the Book of Changes on the floor (as one of Pearl Buck's characters does) since this sacred and holy volume is always treated with reverence and respect.

Among his additional remarks are that cows would not be killed and eaten in China (as Buck claimed), and that tea is always made in China by pouring hot water over the tea leaves and not as Pearl Buck indicated in *The Good Earth* by sprinkling leaves upon the surface of the water. Chinese medicine, Kiang asserts, never included tiger's heart and dog's tooth. In short, he finds that Buck has performed a disservice to the Chinese and to China even though she was reared there and still, he emphasizes, lives there. Yet despite this admission of Buck's closeness to the Chinese scene, Kiang stresses at least three times in his article that Pearl Buck is a foreign writer and ipso facto does not know enough about China to write accurately about the country and its people.

In the same issue of the paper, the *New York Times* allowed Buck to publish a rebuttal to Professor Kiang Kang-Hu's essay.[8] Pearl Buck discusses Kiang's charges in general and point by point. Taking the suicide episode, Buck declares that she herself was present when the woman was taken down from the beam on which she had hanged herself. When the woman was removed from the beam, she was still warm; so a messenger was dispatched at once to summon priests in order to attempt to recall her soul.

Further, Buck asserts that she did see the Book of Changes dropped to the floor although she knows that theoretically sacred religious books should not be thus treated. She states that in many parts of China cows are frequently killed and that she received the tiger's heart and dog's tooth prescription in a medicine shop. She records that tea is scarce in *The Good Earth* locale; therefore, tea in the Northern China region with which she is most familiar is made by placing a few leaves upon the surface of hot water.

She is willing to admit that local practices and customs differ considerably in China, that what may be done in one region or locale may not be done in another area. Nevertheless, in the areas with which she is acquainted, she asserts the accuracy of her portrayal of the customs of those regions. She further emphasizes that she often double-checked details with inhabitants of these areas by reading her descriptions to Chinese friends who could verify data.

Pearl Buck indicates that she is quite familiar with Professor Kiang's attitude. He wants China to be represented to the eyes of the Western world by its scholars and intellectuals—not by its peasants and common people. Buck emphasizes the gulf between the intellectuals and the ordinary people of China. She says that traditionally it has caused mistreatment and inconsideration for the feelings and needs of the proletariat. She regards it as a tragedy that the Chinese intellectuals tend to be ashamed of the common people and to ignore, as much as possible, their existence.

Pearl Buck's defense of her portrayal of Chinese life is immensely effective.[9] In the long history of China a gap has always existed between the Chinese intellectuals and the ordinary men and women who make up the bulk of the population. In general, these intellectuals not only look down upon the common man, but they do not even know the common man. Many of these scholars have been educated at foreign universities, and this training and background often drives them further away from the peasant classes. In an article on the "foreign Chinese" written for the *Yale Review*, Buck notes that when Chinese intellectuals go abroad they frequently give an exaggerated impression of China.[10] They tend to emphasize culture, Confucianism, and the deeply spiritual elements found in Far Eastern philosophy. They also present a distorted picture of the ordinary Chinese peasant. Contrary to the propaganda of the intellectuals, Pearl Buck maintains that Chinese life is much more fundamental and earthy than the principles of Confucianism would indicate. The common man in China is emotional, outgoing, often quarrelsome, with a definitely basic and normal interest in sex and other down-to-earth matters. Buck concludes that the typical Chinese is no more influenced by Confucian principles than the typical American is influenced by the principles of Christ. From the time of the attacks on the validity of *The Good Earth*, Pearl Buck herself confessed a dislike of limited intellectuals who stressed only the Confucian aspects of Chinese life and ignored the common people.

So strong was the feeling engendered against *The Good Earth* by intellectuals, such as Younghill Kang and Kiang Kang-Hu, that even to this day the suspicion exists in certain American critical quarters that Buck has not portrayed Chinese peasant life with accuracy. Such thinking has accepted, without investigation, propaganda attempts by Chinese governmental and intellectual groups to hide the real China from the eyes of the West. Such attempts are legion. Buck herself records several instances. When, for example, a European dignitary visited China in the 1920s, matting was placed on both sides of the street in certain sections of Nanking so that the poor people and the slums would be hidden from his view.[11] On another occasion, news accounts of the making of the movie of *The Good Earth* in China revealed that the Chinese government would not allow people to appear in a certain scene in the picture in rags and bare feet because this episode would give the Western world a false picture of Chinese life.[12]

The Chinese authorities also wanted a tractor used instead of the traditional water buffalo, although at that time there were practically no tractors in China.[13] In the same vein many Chinese deny that the practice of binding women's feet still occurred in the 1920s; yet, again, experience refutes this claim.[14] On one occasion Chinese students in New York City gave a dinner for Pearl Buck and asked her at that time not to publish her translation of *Shui Hu Chuan* because the story contained a cannibal scene which these students felt would give Western readers a disrespectful view of Chinese life.[15] In the attack on the accuracy of *The Good Earth* by certain Chinese critics, we witness a literary manifestation of these same tendencies.

Once and for all, the validity of Pearl Buck's image of China as seen in such novels as *The Good Earth* should be maintained. The philosopher Lin Yutang and other native-born Chinese have defended the novel's accuracy, and additional evidence is available to support such testimony.[16]

II   *"Heresy" and the Foreign Missions*

Not to be forgotten in all the fame and publicity attendant on *The Good Earth* was the fact that its author was a missionary. She was not a missionary in the formal religious-ritual sense, but she was a teacher, as well as the wife of an agricultural missionary, and the daughter of missionary parents.

Moving about in such a religiously oriented society, Pearl Buck naturally possessed a keen interest in missionary activity and in the problems and characteristics of this field of spiritual endeavor. She, therefore, determined to speak out on the missionary question. If she had been an unknown Presbyterian missionary, her comments would not have received the public attention given to the ideas of a world-famous author.

In the early 1930s a study of the foreign mission field was made by fifteen prominent churchmen headed by Dr. W. Ernest Hocking, Professor of Philosophy at Harvard. This group published a report, the Laymen's Foreign Mission Inquiry, which immediately caused much controversy. One of its recommendations was that the modern missionary should make a thorough attempt to acquaint himself or herself with the other religions with which he came in contact and make every effort to associate "kindred" aspects of these religions with his own.

Pearl Buck defended and praised the Laymen's report in an article in *The Christian Century*,[17] later reprinted in pamphlet form.[18] In this essay Pearl Buck maintains that the missionary is too often judged by the total number of converts he makes and by the thrift he demonstrates in handling money allotted to the missions. She asserts that missionaries are restricted unduly by finicky, unwarranted rules and regulations. Moreover, she insists that the missionary should be judged not on doctrinal emphasis but on the honest, proper, and sincere manner of his life—on his Christ-like behavior—and that in the future a greater emphasis should be placed on sending specialists to foreign mission fields. Doctors, nurses, agricultural authorities, mining experts, and other trained personnel are especially needed. Doctrinal considerations and religious proselytizing should be, she argues, a subordinate and de-emphasized function.

Her support for the Laymen's Foreign Mission report angered its many opponents and formed a prelude to her article in the January, 1933, issue of *Harper's* in which she discussed the missionary life in some detail.[19] This essay, soon issued as a pamphlet by her publishers, achieved wide distribution.[20] Buck's beginning comments on the question of foreign missions exploded like a bombshell:

I have seen the missionary narrow, uncharitable, unappreciative, ignorant. I have seen him so filled with arrogance in his own beliefs, so sure that all truth was with him and him only, that my heart has knelt with a humble one before the shrine of Buddha rather than before the God of that missionary, if that God could be true. I have seen missionaries, orthodox missionaries in good standing in the church—abominable phrase:—so lacking in sympathy for the people they were supposed to be saving, so scornful of any civilization except their own, so harsh in their judgments upon one another, so coarse and insensitive among a sensitive and cultivated people that my heart has fairly bled with shame. I can never have done with my apologies to the Chinese people that in the name of a gentle Christ we have sent such people to them.[21]

Further, she avers that some of the missionaries sent to China were mediocre, some superstitious. One missionary admitted to her that he had told his Chinese congregation that their parents and ancestors had gone to hell.

While some of the missionaries exhibit these various weaknesses, the fault is not theirs alone. The church authorities bear much of the responsibility for this situation. Buck cites the case of an agricultural missionary who went to China to help the people there, but whose work was constantly impeded and misunderstood since the church officials put their emphasis on preaching the gospel rather than on economic and agricultural improvement. Church authorities regard the farming techniques and programs as a lure or bait to interest the people in church doctrine and regulations. The church's desire for concrete religious results forces many missionaries to be interested only in adding to church numbers. Ritual and formalism too often take the place of Christian generosity and kind-heartedness. Buck emphasizes that she does not blame the missionaries themselves for their attitude. Church administrators have not, she charges, screened missionary candidates carefully enough and have not brought their ministers to realize the importance of practiced Christian virtues.

The ideas expressed by Pearl Buck in "Is There a Case for Foreign Missions?" are central to much of her thought. She remembers that the missionary group in which she was reared was limited and narrow in viewpoint and often contentious, and that as a child she often fled from this background and preferred to associate with the Chinese people who were much more sympathetic and kind, though supposedly heathen.[22] She also remembers looking at the statue of a goddess of mercy in a Buddhist temple and reflecting on what she had been taught about a harsh and severe Old Testament God. Looking at the Buddhist goddess of mercy, the young girl thought to herself that she preferred the Buddhist goddess because of the kind, understanding expression on her face.[23]

While these thoughts might seem to preclude an affirmative or encouraging viewpoint about Christian missionary activity, Buck argues that there is a case for the foreign missions since Christianity tends to take care of the sick and to give shelter and comfort to those who are in need of such protection. She stresses that Christlike behavior and assistance are the vital manifestations of genuine Christianity and concludes, "let the spirit of Christ be manifested by mode of life rather than by preaching."[24]

"Is There a Case for Foreign Missions?" aroused considerable controversy, and charges of heresy were formally brought against Buck by Dr. J. Gresham Machen, a professor at the Westminster Theological Seminary of Philadelphia. This controversy between Presbyterian modernists and fundamentalists precipitated much argument in the press.[25] The Presbyterian Board of Foreign Missions also came under attack. As a result of Dr. Machen's charge and the ensuing dispute, Pearl Buck submitted her resignation as a missionary of the Presbyterian Church. The Board of Foreign Missions accepted her resignation "with regret."[26] She soon returned to China with her husband, but the debate lingered on in the United States for some time thereafter.

In a magazine article written at this time Pearl Buck stressed the importance of a humanitarian but creedless faith.[27] She affirmed the value of Christ as a pattern of behavior and as an inspiration but rejected any elements of the miraculous or supernatural attached to Christ's life. She noted that many people who profess to believe in the doctrines of Christ often do not practice what they presumably believe. During this same period she remarked that missionary influence in China had been beneficial from an educational and medical point of view, but she held that missionary activities had been ill advised in attempting to break up cultural patterns that had stood the test of centuries.[28]

From the foregoing discussion the genesis and development of Buck's religious beliefs may be observed. Like many sensitive individuals, she could not reconcile the difference between religious theory and practice. She recalled that she did not like white ministers preaching morality in Asia when she remembered the injustice of the white man in the Far East. And so in 1954 she claimed she could not become a church member in the United States for she knew that blacks would not be welcomed in many of these churches.[29] She was interested in deeds not words; in humanitarianism, not dogma. She advocated a religion that stressed brotherhood and assistance to one's fellowman by emphasizing works of justice, kindness, and mercy.

III   House of Earth *Trilogy*

Pearl Buck's intention in *The Good Earth* was to trace the rise of a Chinese family, and she hoped in future novels to follow subsequent generations of this family's activities, particularly after it separated itself from the land. She was inclined to feel that after a wealthy Far-Eastern family deserted the land, it had a tendency to become decadent and to disintegrate.[30] Buck carried on her study of the house of Wang Lung in two novels—*Sons* (1932) and *A House Divided* (1935). In 1935 *The Good Earth* and these two later novels were published as a trilogy called *House of Earth*.

Sons commences with Wang Lung on his deathbed. When Wang looked upon the two sons who were at his bedside, he knew that they wanted him to die, and he was certain too that the time for his passing was near. Wang the Eldest is a wealthy landlord; Wang the Second, a successful merchant; and the youngest son, who does not arrive home until after the death of his father, a military officer.

After the death of Wang Lung, his property is divided. The youngest son (eventually called Wang the Tiger) desires only money; he wants neither house nor land. Nevertheless, in addition to the silver he receives, he is given the old earthen farmhouse in which Wang Lung began his climb to fortune. *Sons* focuses principally on the youthful Wang the Third, while both the older brothers are obvious types. The oldest son is an indolent, pleasure-loving weakling; Wang the Second is a crafty, conniving, thrifty entrepreneur. Neither especially arouses the reader's interest, and both are kept mostly in the background except to assist Wang the Tiger financially in his enterprises and to underscore the decadence and narrowness into which Wang Lung's descendants have fallen.

Wang the Tiger, on the other hand, is zealous, dedicated, and ascetic, reminiscent of his father in his early, productive years. Unlike his father, however, Wang the Tiger hates the land; he intends to become a powerful military figure. Through his own cunning and initiative, and with the money received from his father's estate and with the financial assistance of his brothers, he rises in authority and takes over the leadership of an independent band of soldiers. Yet Wang the Tiger does not become an ordinary bandit. He and his followers overwhelm a puissant outlaw leader; and, with the aid of the local magistrate, they set themselves up as the legal and official troop contingent for that section of northern China. Thus Wang the Tiger possesses the authority of the state for everything he does, and he can tax, conquer further territory, and extend his influence. His area of control, however, is fairly limited: he can eventually control only a part of a large Chinese province. The relationship between the Tiger and his son furnishes the principal interest in the remaining section of the novel.

As a novel, *Sons* labors under the handicap that all sequels to famous books must face. A narrative to equal *The Good Earth* would have to be more powerful and absorbing than *Sons*. Yet, within its own limitations, *Sons* is an interesting, worthwhile novel and a work of no mean effort. It perhaps suffers in that the emphasis on brigands and warlords, on their characteristics and activities, seems somewhat remote to a Western audience.

In all fairness it should be reported that the depredations and pillaging of bandits and warlords had always played an important part in Chinese life. The warlord is one of the most common and ubiquitous figures in the history of China. The famous Chinese novel *Shui Hu Chuan*, earlier translated into English by Pearl Buck herself, is constructed around the activities of a band of brigands.[31] In Buck's autobiographical writings the movements and attacks of various bandit groups are often recorded. Warlords continually fought among themselves, as well as attacked homes and villages. Such happenings were always a part of existence in China, and everyone soon learned to live among such upheavals.[32] Even when Buck lived in Nanking, the area was ruled by a warlord named Sun Chuan-fang, and China at that time was largely divided into sections under the control of such military figures.[33] In the very same year in which *Sons* was published, the *New York Times* carried a news account of a Chinese warlord named the White Tiger, who may have served in part as a model for Wang the Tiger.[34]

Cornelia Spencer reports that *Sons* was Pearl Buck's own personal favorite of all her many books about life in China.[35] Part of this preference is doubtless due to an author's normal reaction against the excessive one-book emphasis on the part of critics and the reading public. Some of this favoritism, however, must be attributed to the fact that Buck saw the bandit chief and warlord as one of the most characteristic aspects of Chinese life. To write convincingly of such a figure, however, is a difficult task. One remembers Pablo in *For Whom the Bell Tolls* and the revolutionist Braggioni in Katherine Anne Porter's *The Flowering Judas*; but well-drawn, realistic outlaw-type characters by American authors are few.

The fundamental defect of *Sons* is the weakness of the characterization of Wang the Tiger. In a magazine article on "Chinese War Lords," Pearl Buck gives an interesting and informative view of the wide variety and the distinctiveness of such men.[36] One such figure was Feng Yu Hsiang. Feng Yu Hsiang controlled his own region in northwestern China, but he frequently moved into national affairs. In 1924, for example, he attacked Peking and imprisoned Ts'ao K'un, the president of the country. In 1926 he fought against the Nationalist forces, and in the following year he concluded an agreement with Chiang Kai-shek, arriving in Nanking and boldly declaring his support at a student assembly. Two years later Feng Yu Hsiang severed relations with Chiang and established his own government in Peking.

In appearance Feng Yu Hsiang was a large, thick-set, domineering figure—a man filled with power and authority—moody, unpredictable, treacherous, and yet at the same time filled with humor, seeming good will, and considerable personal charm. Although he boasted of his simplicity, he was a complex figure with a great flair for the dramatic. At one time he was a Christian, at another, a Communist, and he was usually the unceasing opponent of any government not his own. He was an excellent military leader with well-trained followers, and he appealed to both peasants and intellectuals. He was mentally alert and intelligent, but uneducated because of his peasant background. Yet, on one occasion, he took a chemistry course at the University of Nanking because he believed that science might renew China.

Another warlord, Wu Pei Fu, eventually retired from military activity in order to study Buddhist philosophy; nevertheless, he continued to maintain his army. Pearl Buck records the personality of such men as Feng Yu Hsiang and Wu Pei Fu, their individuality, their imaginative and dramatic deeds, and their ability to become legends, creating an aura of the old heroic times.

In contrast to such figures, Wang the Tiger is a considerably more limited and colorless individual. Although the reader comes to know him quite well, a particular remoteness about him persists. His motives and behavior are analyzed at some length, but he does not arouse interest or sympathy as Wang Lung and O-lan do.

While early in the novel Wang the Tiger appears to possess the necessary dedication and strength of will to be a great military leader, the reader discovers in time that he is too tender-hearted to be a really successful warlord. The distressed and starving people of a southern city arouse his sorrow and compassion, and he finds the looting and barbarian behavior of his own victorious army distasteful. He can be ruthless only when he is angry, and his anger is often feigned and transitory. Near the end of *Sons* he acknowledges his unfitness for the role he is playing when he mumbles, "I am too weak—I am always too weak—after all, I am too weak for a lord of war—."[37]

Another significant—although touching—sign of his weakness in the role of a ruthless leader is his excessive devotion to his own son. The child intensifies Tiger's conviction to increase his domain and to continue his gains so that further territory may eventually pass on to the son's control. Yet, at the same time, the presence of the son weakens Wang since he does not wish to let the boy out of his sight. The Tiger watches over the boy's education and training and seeks his companionship whenever possible. An inborn cautious and conservative bent, which prevents Tiger from making more daring forays and from increasing his power and prestige to really significant heights, is intensified by his becoming so wrapped up in the boy's development that he does practically nothing to increase his personal military and political influence. So engrossed in the lad is he that nothing else matters too much.

Much of Wang the Tiger's interest in his son is the result of his own sexual frustration. In *The Good Earth* the serving girl Pear Blossom attracted his interest, but Wang Lung in his old age took her for a concubine, which triggered Wang the Tiger's departure from his father's house. When Wang the Tiger eventually falls in love, it is with the mistress of a rival bandit leader. Wang kills this robber chief and takes the woman for his wife. Although he truly loves her and demonstrates deep affection, he learns that she has betrayed him by trying to set up a competing military force. In hurt and heated anger he kills his wife and reaches a state of complete disillusionment about women. Although he later takes two wives, he does so only that they may furnish him with children. He desires no further contact with them and ignores them completely. The place that a woman might have taken in his heart and mind is now taken by his son. (His daughters he neglects shamefully.)

When he analyzes his brothers' sons, his determination to mold his own son intensifies. The older sons of the eldest Wang, Wang the Landlord, are very much like their father; they are dissolute, well-dressed, well-groomed rakes, interested in sexual pleasure and in epicurean living. The sons of Wang the Merchant are clerks who are apprenticed in business, but they are lazy and shiftless when their father is not about. They look forward to his death because they will have plenty of money to spend and to do as they please. Wang the Merchant is himself so absorbed in money-making concerns that he does not see his own sons for what they are. Wang the Tiger, who hates indolence and loose living, determines that his son will be reared ascetically and developed into a disciplined, well-trained soldier and military leader.

To this end Wang the Tiger gives his son Yuan every advantage. The young lad is given a splendid foreign gun and a magnificent steed, he receives military tutoring and schooling, and his whole life is centered around soldiery and warfare. Yet Wang cannot understand why Yuan responds to these things with silent discontent. He thinks "what more can he want! He has all I dreamed of when I was his age and more than I dreamed."[38] But, just as Wang the Tiger in his desire to be a military leader had rejected everything his father stood for, so too Yuan rejects his father. Yuan is fascinated only by the changes of nature, by the growing of crops, by the life of the ordinary farmer. He does not possess the heart for army activity, nor does he have any particular interest in military matters. Like many determined and shortsighted parents, Wang the Tiger refuses to understand or accept this situation. As a result, he is thoroughly disillusioned when Yuan withdraws from military school. Even though Yuan's return signifies his love for his father—he has rejected the importunities of South China military leaders to join in the elimination of warlords—his father cannot understand how his son could think of him as a mere bandit chief or how Yuan could propose to retire for a time to his grandfather's old farmhouse. This act is the supreme irony and the supreme disillusionment for Wang the Tiger: the old brigand can feel the rejected hand of his own father reaching out from his grave and laying claim to his grandson. Wang the Tiger now has become thoroughly frustrated in his goals and dreams, for Yuan has also made him realize that he was never an important warlord.[39] Nevertheless, the Tiger attempts to cling to a little self-respect by insisting that he was never a robber. So steeped in these feelings and so shattered is Wang that his son's gesture of love in returning home and his spoken words of affection are completely lost.[40]

The final scene is a pitiful revelation of one man's awareness of failure and frustration. The conflict between father and son again presents itself just as it had existed in the relationship between Wang the Tiger and his own father. Wang has never fully known and understood himself before; neither has he known nor understood his only beloved son. Yet with all this revelation Wang the Tiger does not mean as much to us as he should. He has the problems of a major character, but he does not come alive as a major character ought to do. Wang appears to be too easily self-deceived, and too naïve. He is also too reserved, aloof, and forbidding. He possesses a ruling passion which can evoke little support, and even his passionate love for the brigand's paramour seems obviously ill-advised and rather foolish. In short, the portrayal of Wang contains little to bring reader identification; and even his ultimate despair, which is basically the result of his own foolishness and naïveté, seems deserved and rather fitting. It is difficult to sense tragedy here, at least from the way the story and characters are presented.

The style of *Sons* follows the same biblical-Chinese saga influence displayed in *The Good Earth* and, in general, repeats this pattern beneficially. Many of the long sweeping sentences are especially lyrical and mellifluous, and numerous passages of thoughtful beauty recur. During the death scene and the burial ceremonial section the writing has an effective stateliness and ornament. In the episodes involving the rise and adventures of Wang the Tiger, the poetic prose, which the movement of time and the seasons brought to *The Good Earth*, is not so pronounced. In *The Good Earth* the style was absorbed in the humanity of the characters and their difficulties; consequently, the style took on a special life and feeling. In *Sons* Wang the Tiger does not maintain the same interest to carry along the style with him. Thus, the prose of *Sons* occasionally seems utilitarian, a mere archaic-flavored ordering and recital of events. While it may not be determined that Pearl Buck felt her story and people more deeply and more vibrantly in *The Good Earth* than in *Sons*, this conclusion is strongly suggested by the style and characterization of *Sons*.

Sons, of course, possesses social and historical value as an illustration of a way of life in China. The reader learns and understands how warlords spring up, how they consolidate their power, and how they relate to the people, to governmental figures, and to rival bandit chiefs. The novel also has merit as a pointed, ironic commentary on the differences between generations in the same family. Not only are the differences in view toward life and the land decidedly impressed, but other contrasts are vividly underscored. Wang the Tiger's share of his father's land, for example, is sold in order to increase his military buying power; yet Wang Lung had hated war and soldiers and deplored military activity. The individual differences between Wang Lung's sons and their wives display a universality which rings true and is an easily remembered aspect of the story.

But, in the final analysis, *Sons* falls short of *The Good Earth* because it does not have the same universal quality of timelessness, the same inevitable moment of birth and death, of success and failure, of tragedy and of joy. Universality has been narrowed to the rise of a warlord and the subsequent—but never powerfully felt by the reader—misunderstanding between father and son. Even the time movement of Wang Lung's descendants seems to sink into secondary significance because of the emphasis given to the story of one rather colorless military chief.

In *A House Divided*, the final volume of the trilogy, the emphasis is placed on Wang the Tiger's son Yuan. The novel begins just after Yuan's quarrel with his father. Yuan is nineteen years old at this time and quite immature. His emotions are mixed, and he is prone to self-pity. He realizes that his father has centered all his love on him, but he dwells on the belief that his father has never truly loved him because he has always dominated and tried to force his wishes upon him. He is further irked because the Tiger does not understand or appreciate the choice Yuan made in deserting the revolutionists and returning to him. Guilt feelings and regrets that he deserted his military school comrades who claimed to serve the common people also distress Yuan. Cut off now from both his father and his school companions, Yuan feels isolated and completely alone.

In this condition he decides to flee from his father and the revolutionary army, and he seeks as his refuge the most tranquil place he has ever known—the old earthen house from which his grandfather Wang Lung started on the road to affluence and position. When Yuan travels to his grandfather's house, one of the farmers informs him that his choice of a hiding place is unwise, and in a few words the present condition of Wang Lung's descendants is related:

Your honored father is not loved well because he is a lord of war, and your uncles are not loved, either. . . . Sir, the people on the land here so hated your elder uncle that he and his lady grew afraid and with their sons they went to a coastal city to live where foreign soldiers keep the peace, and when your second uncle comes to collect the rents, he comes with a band of soldiers he has hired from the town![41]

The area where Wang Lung worked diligently and was honored and respected has, through the behavior of his three sons, become an unsafe dwelling place for his grandson.

Yuan idealizes the farmer's life on the land, but the people who live adjacent to his grandfather's house cannot comprehend his meaning. To them, their life is one of difficulty and hardship. After a short stay at his grandfather's home, Yuan learns that the Tiger is dying; he must return to his father's headquarters. Wang the Tiger is not dying, but he appears to have aged suddenly and is certainly ill. Yuan's fear of his father's anger and feigned spells of fury diminishes, and Yuan realizes that his father was never ruthless nor harsh enough to be an important warlord. Wang demands that Yuan marry a woman chosen by his parents so that the Tiger may look forward to the birth of descendants—a demand that infuriates Yuan because he wishes to choose his own wife according to the new manner of marriage arrangement.

Yuan again leaves the Tiger's home, travels to Shanghai, and lives in the fashionable home of his half-sister Ai-lan and her mother. There Yuan goes to school and moves in the wealthy circles of Chinese city life. He reluctantly learns how to dance, goes to parties and elaborate balls, and mingles with the privileged classes. Wang the Eldest and his family now live in Shanghai and move about in these circles. One of Wang's sons, Sheng, is a poet and a fashionable man about town, but a younger brother is a student revolutionist. The contrast between life of the wealthy and life of the poor in Shanghai is strikingly explored, and the division between the two groups is severe and extreme. The most beggared and abject povery exists side by side with extravagance and the most luxurious indolence. The revolutionary group is active, however, particularly among the students. His cousin Meng insists that Yuan join his revolutionary group. Only when the rich are displaced and the poor raised can there be justice in China, Meng argues. Meng hates intensely; he hates not only the rich, but foreigners and Eurasians, and, as time proves, he even hates the backwardness and docility of the poor. When Wang the Tiger tries to force his son to marry the parental choice, Yuan in a fit of anger joins the revolutionists. He now feels that his father represents part of the old way of life which must be destroyed.

When the revolution erupts and its armies move up from the south, known revolutionaries in Shanghai are rounded up by the authorities, imprisoned, and soon executed. Yuan is betrayed by a girl student whose devotion he has rejected, and he is jailed. Heavy bribes are paid; and he and Sheng, the poet, who has been implicated, are smuggled aboard a ship and eventually arrive in America.

Yuan lives in the United States for six years, studying diligently, winning scholastic honors, and achieving his doctoral degree. His admiration for America's material achievements is tempered by the racial prejudice he encounters, by weird notions Americans hold about the Chinese, and by discourtesy. Yuan assumes a defensive posture. He becomes a chauvinistic Chinese and brags of his country, remembering only the good things. He thinks of the riches of the Chinese coastal cities, the fine houses, the many automobiles; he forgets the farmers and the poverty-stricken villages. He publicly contradicts an American missionary who speaks of famines in China, of the many beggars and lepers, and of the deliberate killing of baby girls. Yuan stresses the great philosophers of the past and their exaltation of wisdom and reason; he emphasizes the many fine elements of Chinese life. His chauvinistic attitude leads him to disparage America further, although the achievements of the United States force him into an ambivalent attitude.

While his cousin Sheng mixes well into American life and continues to be a fashionable and sought-after social butterfly, Yuan's life in the United States is, for the most part, lonely and isolated. He does manage to establish a close relationship with one of his college professors. Yuan visits Dr. Wilson's home frequently and becomes friendly with his wife and daughter Mary. Mary is attracted to him. She is a bright, sensitive type who loves and admires China. These qualities are blended, however, with a certain American hardness, assurance, and domineering attitude. Consequently, she alternately attracts and repels Yuan. His relationship with women has always been rather unsatisfactory. Aloofness, shyness, and timidity, mingling with the knowledge of his father's misogynist attitude and the remembrance that both his father and he have been betrayed by women, have scarred Yuan's feelings. When he kisses Mary Wilson at her request, he finds the physical contact unpleasant; and the ensuing feeling of distaste he experiences is based on the fact that she is not of his own race.

During Yuan's stay in the United States a new revolution has taken place in China, and upon his return to his homeland he finds this new movement in control. When his ship sails into harbor, Yuan feels proud of his native land; but he is immediately depressed by the beggars and poor who crowd around the dock. Later, on a journey inland to visit his father, he is struck with distaste for the poor, ordinary Chinese. What he had forgotten in America and what he had tended to idealize in former years are now brought before him with frightful clarity. He is ashamed and embarrassed by the poverty of many of his countrymen. He is glad that he did not marry Mary Wilson and bring her to China. Then her dreams of his homeland would have been shattered. It is better, he thinks, for her to remember the dreams and not know the truth. Yet these are his people, they are part of his blood, he cannot deny them, they still have claims upon him.

Yuan finds his father in decline. The Tiger's army is shattered, and the old man has little but braggadocio left. Soon he is overcome and tortured by another bandit chief, and he dies in Yuan's presence.

In the meantime, Yuan has gone to work in the capital of the new government. A modern city is in the process of construction, new ideas are being tried, and Yuan participates in the general progress by teaching in a government school. His cousin Meng, who had been a member of the previous revolutionary movement, is now a captain in the military forces of the new government. Meng is still cynical about the ability of the poor to be worthy of the revolution, but he does hold out hope for their children. Meng even chafes under the present leaders, and he predicts a newer revolution in the future when equality and justice will reign. He is already laying plans to join a new revolutionary group which will form in western China and which will equalize rich and poor.

The times are thus in ferment. New forces are shaping China, and foreign influences are strong. The young will play an important role in future developments. Yuan comes finally to think out his place in this pattern. He could not fit into his grandfather's earthen house. It still attracts him to some extent, but he has grown beyond its limitations. Yet, at the same time, he is not at home in the fashionable world of Wang the Eldest, of Sheng, of his half-sister Ai-lan; they are too foreign, too unnatural. He realizes that he is in the lonely middle ground between Wang Lung's earthen house and his eldest uncle's foreign home. Since he cannot surrender his tie to the past, he must accept the people of China as they are, acknowledge both past and present, and look to the future with maturity and a more balanced hope of improvements to come. China is now on a middle ground, halfway between the past and the future.

A House Divided, which studies the development of one young man's mind during a turbulent and crucial period of modern Chinese history and probes the changes wrought in one family over several generations, is the weakest volume in the *House of Earth* trilogy. Part of the reason for this situation is that Yuan does not hold the same reader interest as did Wang Lung or even Wang the Tiger. Yuan does not come alive as a believable individual. None of the characters in *A House Divided* arouses any particular interest; and, while much happens, the events do not involve the reader in the action.

As an examination of one man's mind, *A House Divided* fails to be appealing primarily because Buck's technique is not thorough and conclusive enough in its introspective probing. Yuan seems to wear his heart on his sleeve, and his sudden shifts of emotion and feeling are not presented logically. One moment he loves his father, then he hates the father, then again he loves, then he returns to hating, etc. In sudden hatred he joins the revolutionists, although he has a distaste for war and military activity. He admires America; then he hates America; then a blend of these feelings occurs, with dislike predominating. Later, while he is teaching, we are told that he does not care for his pupils. Three pages later we discover that he is deeply concerned and interested in the students. This sudden and frequent vacillation denotes an emotionally unstable individual who is unworthy of genuine reader concern. Granted that Yuan is maturing, that he is groping toward a more adult awareness of his place and his world, his chameleon-like shifts of mood lessen our respect for him and weaken our belief in his reality.

Perhaps Yuan must share his fault with the storytelling technique employed. Buck's technique is more effective in analyzing external events and elements than in presenting internal aspects. Too much explaining of Yuan's thoughts and character occurs. The reader is told about too many of these changes in emotion without being prepared for such variations of mood. The author should have led up to more of these alterations and smoothed the way. Yuan's shifts in viewpoint, often too abrupt and too pronounced, seem exceptionally inconsistent; and they jar and scatter the novel's totality of impact.

The reader is also too conscious of authorial manipulation in the handling of Yuan's character. He is a puppet who dances the same tunes on constantly shifting strings, strings which are observed by the audience. The romance between Yuan and Mei-ling is, for instance, shamelessly managed and rigged by the author. The satellite characters in *A House Divided* suffer a similar fate.

Further, the structure of the novel is not clearly defined. *A House Divided* treats of a number of places and a number of events, and its canvas often becomes episodic and unwieldy. Malcolm Cowley has observed that the material in this last volume of the trilogy is too scattered and does not progress to any significant conclusion.[42] He notes that Buck intended in part to demonstrate how Wang Lung's original vitality was dissipated in various descendants and into various locales. Cowley points out that the China described in *A House Divided* is separated into different groups and lingers between past and present conditions with the future unknown and uncertain.[43]

Under these conditions a unified novel is practically an impossibility. Cowley argues further that the conflicts in the plot are not dramatic, and he makes a plausible case for this conclusion.

Buck's style, effective in the early scenes when Yuan returns to his grandfather's earthen house, often appears flat and ordinary—a mere recording of events. The prose of *A House Divided* is, in general, much too dull and undistinguished to do more than merely tell a story. A particularly heavy burden is placed on the style to describe internal events; and while at times some poetry filters through the external description, the style is not adequate to the needs of so much internal analysis. It also falls flat in the sections dealing with Yuan's adventures in America. While often appropriate and picturesque in relation to farm or rural description, Buck's style loses effectiveness in its rendering of life in a big city such as Shanghai and in its picturing of scenes in the United States. In this connection the prose seems lifeless and even tired, and its simplicities are out of harmony with the portrayal of a more modern, dynamic mode of existence. It is, of course, true that the episodic choppiness of *A House Divided* places a strain on the style. As a result, it loses much of its sweep and stately flow, rendering it less poetic and less meaningful than in the first two books of the trilogy.

A House Divided has appeal as the final view of a family that we have seen at its best and at its worst. The descendants of land-orientated Wang Lung have scattered in all directions. One branch lives almost as foreigners, moving in the height of metropolitan fashion and comfort; another represents crafty, pragmatic commercial interests. One descendant is now an embittered revolutionist looking forward to new political upheavals; another, Yuan himself, stands between the old, stolid, rural ways of Wang Lung and the new foreign influences and trends. This is China near the end of the 1920s, a country in transition at a time of ferment. One revolution just finished, the seeds of another growing; a time of confusion and unrest on the land; the increasing Westernization of customs and behavior patterns in the large cities; a way of life that is completely out of keeping with the old ways on the land; a new generation searching and trying to find itself—all of these factors are decidedly valid in any portrayal of the twentieth-century development of China. Yet, while such events themselves have great significance, the people in *A House Divided* who participate in them appear pallid and lifeless in comparison.

IV   The Mother

In 1934, between the publication of the second and third volumes of her *House of Earth* trilogy, Pearl Buck issued one of her most unusual novels, *The Mother*. This narrative was intended to give a universal portrait of the eternal mother, to present the various cycles of her life, and to capture some of the timelessness of her existence. In a sense, this novel was attempting to describe one woman in the same manner that *The Good Earth* had endeavored to analyze one particular family.

The mother of the title is a young Chinese farmer's wife who works side by side with her husband on the land. Her aged and almost blind mother-in-law lives with the couple. In addition to helping in the fields, the mother cares for the family and performs the numerous household duties of any wife. The mother is young, and although her life is strenuous and difficult, she possesses a vigorous zest to relieve its monotony.

But her husband, two years younger, is not so patient and adaptable. He is extremely unhappy with his life on the farm, although bred to it from youth. He is undisciplined, very handsome, and quite lucky at gambling, in which he participates at night in the little hamlet. He longs for life in the large cities far from his present location.

A peddler who sells the husband a pretentious robe the family cannot afford brings discontent to a boil. The purchase money consists of three silver coins treasured by the wife because they are a wedding present from her own mother. The wife did not wish to part with these coins. Yet the husband ("one who loved his pleasure . . . a lad held down to life he was not ready for") took the money forcibly and purchased the clothing.[44] This incident leads to a coolness between husband and wife. There had been quarrels and disputes before, but this was their most serious rift. Soon the husband deserts his wife.

To save face, the mother tells her neighbors that her husband has gone to a distant city to work. She now reaps the rice harvest with some aid from a cousin and performs all her usual household tasks. In time, the mother pretends to receive letters from her husband in order to allay the neighbors' suspicions of desertion.

Her daily life and its tasks continue, but the mother longs to conceive more children. Her strong maternal instincts are thwarted, although her husband has provided her with several children. The land agent perceives the mother's loneliness, discontent, and longing. Eventually the two come together in sexual union, but only on one occasion. After the intercourse the agent is no longer interested in her; however, the mother finds herself pregnant. She takes various medical preparations in order to bring about an abortion, and despite much pain and sickness, her purpose is accomplished.

Later the mother learns from a doctor that her young daughter, who has been suffering from eye trouble for many years, has now become almost completely blind. This situation becomes another arrow to wound the universal mother's heart.

Time moves forward, and the mother no longer feels her youth, although she is now only forty-three years old. She begins to favor her younger son at the expense of her elder one. The elder is a steady and diligent worker, but the younger son, while exceedingly lazy and shiftless, attracts the mother's affection because he is handsome and lighthearted. Soon the older son marries, and his wife comes to live in the mother's house. Now the mother feels superfluous; she has become nothing "but the old woman in the house."[45] To the mother's eyes, it seems apparent that her daughter-in-law does not treat the blind girl well. The mother believes also that her son and his wife have cut themselves off from her.

At last it is decided to betroth the blind girl so that she may have a house of her own. She is, therefore, wed into an impoverished family living in a distant mountainous area. Some time later, when the mother treks to the distant hills to visit her blind daughter, she finds the girl dead under mysterious circumstances. She discovers that the girl's husband was almost witless and that her daughter had been mistreated. The mother can only lament and carry her remorse within her heart.

She grows older and more weary and looks forward to having grandsons. She still has the solace of her comely youngest son; however, he participates in Communist activities, is captured by the authorities and executed. The mother's grief knows no bounds. She is a modern Rachel weeping for her children; "and she would not be comforted, for they were not."

At this propitious moment the mother's first grandchild is born, and the mother's delight is deep and triumphant. This new child gives life, hope, and meaning to the existence of the old woman.

The Mother is an extremely important work in the canon of Pearl Buck's writing. The never-ending cycle of birth and death and the eternal round of a mother's life with its joys and sorrows stir the reader because of their proportions and the novelist's insight into life. Here is a portrait of a perennial mother, with universal implications. A synopsis of the story can give no feeling of its impact, but it can indicate the rhythmical ebb and flow of a mother's existence and the fluctuations of her trials, frustrations, and periods of happiness and contentment.

In many ways *The Mother* is one of Buck's finest books. It possesses many distinctions: for example, the cyclical flow of time, the eternal *mater dolorosa* caught in this movement, the tragedies and hardness of existence, the mistakes and crises revolving around the life of a mortal woman. Nevertheless, in an overall estimate, one comes to admire the book for its ambitious attempt rather than for its complete realization of achievement. Several reasons support this viewpoint.

In the first part of the novel description predominates, and the mother speaks very little. In the latter part, however, she becomes, comparatively at least, quite garrulous and even naggish. While this change is logical under the impact of increasing age and sorrow, it tends to forfeit reader sympathy. The mother also loses the reader's support because she was too neglectful of medical care for her sickly daughter, at times too much of a shrew toward her husband (although much of this feeling is justified because of his conduct), and because she rather arbitrarily favors her younger son over her much more stable and deserving elder son. These failings can be justified on the basis that such events happen in life, but in the novel they tend to emphasize the main character's weaknesses and, hence, to diminish sympathy.

The shift between the first part of the mother's career and her relatively sudden aging (at the beginning of Chapter 13) comes too suddenly and brings forth a feeling of abruptness and imbalance. The reader is, moreover, not thoroughly prepared for the change in the mother's rank and position after the marriage of her elder son, and the full force of the cycle of life and the bafflement this cycle often brings are not captured as meaningfully as possible.

A prime weakness exists in the failure to involve the reader in a sense of the mother's toughness and power of endurance. If one compares the unnamed mother in Pearl Buck's novel with two characters in a somewhat similar plan—Bertolt Brecht's Mother Courage and John Steinbeck's Ma Joad—this failure becomes strikingly apparent. Both Ma Joad and Mother Courage make a more forceful impact; they spring to life and assume reality, being more vividly realized and memorable. They are not without character defects, but their faults do not detract from reader sympathy and involvement. Even in more immediate contrast, the mother does not compare too favorably with O-lan. O-lan is also long-suffering; and, while she is not intended to represent a universal type, she does have many of the qualities of the struggling-but-surviving woman of endurance. The basic fault with the mother is that she becomes too much a type and too little a realized individual. Both Mother Courage and Ma Joad have universal implications of type, but they are also vivid individuals about whom the reader cares.

Pearl Buck seems to feel that her mother character was too far removed from common experience to be popular. In *My Several Worlds* Buck relates that in *The Mother* she attempted to describe the existence of a universal peasant woman, a woman who receives little fulfillment except from the daily events of her life.[46] Readers in Italy and France, where the peasant woman is a well-known figure, appreciated the book, she remarks; but readers in the United States found her principal character remote. Pearl Buck finds this reaction strange because there are many such farming women in various parts of the United States. She also comments on the fact that William Faulkner's weird and demented characters are remote to her experience; but she accepts them because they are the effect of powerful characterization. If characterization is vivid, complete, and penetrating, the strangeness of person and subject matter is conquered. In her portrayal of the mother Buck has not succeeded in rendering her character with accuracy and thorough discernment.[47]

The prose of *The Mother* is reduced to the barest simplicity. It is less rich, poetic, and varied than in *The Good Earth*; it possesses an economy which, while it often approaches biblical phrasing and is often pleasingly lyrical, eventually becomes monotonous. Although the style is deliberately reduced to the utmost simplicity in order to balance with the stark and basic movement of time and with the plight of the universal mother caught in this movement, about halfway through the novel one realizes that the prose is too plain and too sparse for the theme; more richness and variety are needed, more poetry, more of the coloring found in *The Good Earth*. The style in *The Mother* suggests that the biblical-Chinese saga style, which Pearl Buck has often used very effectively, can be drawn too thin or be too simple in a lengthy narrative and, hence, lacks a vital heightening and variety of tone and harmony.

In general, *The Mother* is an interesting, ambitious attempt to effect a monumental achievement in both theme and style. The attempt does not succeed, but the effort was notable. The theme is worthy of a truly great work, and the material is there; but Buck has miscalculated the stylistic effects, and she has not thought out nor developed thoroughly enough the characterization of her central figure. In addition, the reader is told about a great many things happening too suddenly in the universal movement of time. This suddenness is not prepared for and seems incongruous. *The Mother* definitely needed more patient revision.

CHAPTER 4

The Nobel Prize Biographies

M OST general readers and even many literary critics and historians are under the impression that Pearl Buck received the Nobel Prize for *The Good Earth*.[1] This is simply not true. The Nobel Committee citation, which accompanied the award, read: "For rich and generous epic description of Chinese peasant life and masterpieces of biography."[2] Selma Lagerlöf, the Swedish novelist who was the first woman to win the Nobel Prize for Literature and who was a member of the Nobel Committee, revealed that she cast her vote in favor of Pearl Buck because of the excellence of Buck's biography of her father.[3] These two facts indicate the importance of what may be called, with incontrovertible accuracy, the Nobel Prize biographies: *The Exile*, a study of Buck's mother, and *Fighting Angel*, a portrait of her father. Both of these volumes were published in 1936.

I The Exile

The Exile was in fact the first of Pearl Buck's books to be written.[4] Shortly after her mother's death in 1921, Buck began a biography to serve as a family memorial. After its completion, the manuscript reposed on the shelf of a high closet. Later, during the Revolution of 1926–27, Pearl Buck's home in Nanking was looted. Fortunately, the manuscript containing her mother's biography was one of the few things in the house not stolen or destroyed. Later, the text was reworked but was not published until Buck's writing career was well established. Pearl Buck has declared that only the names of the characters have been changed and that everything else about the book is true. In the principal name changes, Caroline is Carie; her husband Absalom, Andrew; and the youthful Pearl, Comfort.

The maiden name of Caroline Sydenstricker, Pearl Buck's mother, was Stulting. The Stultings were Dutch in origin, but, because of religious persecution, the family left Holland and migrated to the United States. At first they settled in Pennsylvania, but there they were cheated in land transactions, and soon they moved on to West Virginia.

Caroline Stulting was a woman of opposing natures. On the one hand, she was a fun-loving, witty, fast-thinking, and extremely personable woman with a quick temper which flared suddenly and usually passed just as quickly. She loved to read, to listen to good music, to garden, to play with her children. She liked to sing and to compose rhymes, and could be completely carefree. On the other hand, a strong puritanical streak ran in her nature. She often sought God and vowed to pray more, to be more devotional. She worried that her more sensual nature would lead her away from God. When she was a mature young woman, she was emotionally and physically attracted to a dashing young man who was desirable in all ways save one. This suitor returned her affection, but she eventually rejected him, and later gave this explanation for her action: "he was not good. He drank and he came from a family that drank. It wasn't easy to be good, and I was afraid if I married him I might grow like him."[5]

When she was a young girl, Caroline Stulting sought a sign from God so that she could believe in Him with more assurance. Caroline determined to give herself completely to God if He would present some sign of His existence. In her distraction she promised that she would become a missionary if God could reassure her. A particularly trying period for her occurred during her mother's fatal sickness. When Caroline's mother came to the moment of death, her last words were, "Why—it's—all *true!*"[6] Caroline assumed that this remark was the long-awaited sign from God. She determined to give herself to God's call.

After her education in West Virginia, she was sent to a young ladies' finishing school near Louisville, Kentucky. When twenty-two, she returned home and broached to her father the idea of her becoming a missionary. He emphatically refused his approval. Absalom Sydenstricker was visiting his brother who was the pastor of Caroline's church. Hearing that this young man desired to be a missionary to China, she introduced herself to him and announced a like intention. The young preacher grew interested in her, and she accepted his eventual proposal of marriage against her father's wishes. Caroline immediately felt religious and exalted; the youthful clergyman touched responsive spiritual chords in her being. They were married July 8, 1880, and almost immediately set out on the trip to China.

Caroline's life in China was anything but satisfying. She and her husband were completely opposite in nature. She hoped for a companionship with him that might join both family interests and their vocational concerns. She found that her husband wanted only someone to perform household duties, not a soulmate who would share his work. Her husband emphasized the doctrine of St. Paul that the woman was to be under the complete subjection of man. His wife, who had a keen mind and was both perceptive and intelligent, chafed under his narrowness and his shortsightedness. She grew to resent her husband's slower pace, his selfishness, and his impracticality.

Caroline's old doubts about God never went away. Four of her seven children died in China, and the chances were that, if they had received adequate medical care or had lived in a more health-conscious country—such as America—their deaths would have been averted. Caroline came to resent what she regarded as sacrifices demanded by God. The poverty, suffering, and misery that she beheld in China also disturbed her belief in a God who would allow such things. Yet she had to settle for a trust that God did exist. She still hoped for a sign, "clinging to her hope of God, because she knew of nothing else in which to believe and faith in some tangible good was essential to her positive nature."[7] Near the end of her life, when she was on her deathbed, she did not want her husband to come near, and she rejected his notion of a strict, angry, and rigid Almighty. She told her daughter at this time: "I believe one ought to choose the happy, bright things of life, like dancing and laughter and beauty. I think if I had it to do over again I would choose those instead of thinking them sinful."[8]

As her realization of the cleavage between her husband and herself deepened, her longing for the United States increased. She always possessed a poignant attachment for her West Virginia birthplace and her family. She continually told her children stories about life in America and made it come alive in their minds. Though she especially looked forward to the furloughs in America, it was a continuing unhappiness to her as the years passed to return to the United States and to find fewer members of her family alive, as well as to discover changes in her home town and in the countryside. She felt that America was cutting itself off from her, forgetting her. In time she became somewhat reconciled to this situation, and she became convinced that at least she could always hold America in memory. But homesickness never deserted her; she was always truly an exile. On one occasion, when Pearl herself wanted to leave her mother for a period of time in order to live and work in another part of China, her mother taxed her with being disloyal to her parents' wishes. Pearl in return reminded her mother that she had disobeyed her own father by marrying a missionary and coming to China. Her mother responded that she should not have disobeyed him; she declared that she had done the wrong thing in rejecting his advice.[9]

Although her personal difficulties over God's existence and her disillusionment with her husband were apparent from time to time, she did all she reasonably could to support her husband's missionary work. Early in her career in China she contracted tuberculosis and was advised to return to America. Rather than follow this medical advice and cause her husband's work to cease, she requested that they be transferred to North China, and there with rest and care and a more favorable climate she overcame her illness. When Absalom desired to make a Chinese translation of the New Testament, Caroline supported his intention; through rigid self-denial and extreme economy, she enabled him to save enough money to publish edition after edition of this translation.[10] When Absalom was near the age of retirement, younger missionaries with new ideas and different ways constantly censured his practices. Yet Caroline defended her husband staunchly, expressing her loyalty and devotion to him in the most ardent manner.[11]

Caroline's adventures in China were often epic and heroic in themselves. During the Boxer Rebellion she and her children had to flee for their lives. On another occasion when Absalom was out on a rural excursion, a mob gathered at the gate of Caroline's house at midnight with the intention of killing her and the children. At that time she, her husband, and their children were the only white people living in the area, and the crowd blamed the white foreigners for a frightful drought which plagued the region. When the mob gathered, Caroline went to the gate, opened it, gathered her children about her, and offered tea to the crowd. The mob—astounded by her bravery, her friendliness, and the innocence of the scene—soon dispersed. Such adventures were just an ordinary part of day-to-day living in late nineteenth- and early twentieth-century China.

Although her husband would have preferred her to tend to her household duties, she took part in as much missionary work as she could, although her work was usually on a more practical basis. She was more interested in the cleanliness and health of the bodies of the Chinese than in their souls. Whenever possible, she ran a small clinic which treated skin infections and other simple illnesses. She tended many sick mothers and sick babies. She was always on call to discuss and to help Chinese women with medical and domestic problems.

She taught school frequently and emphasized cleanliness and other health measures among her students; but she worried that, in her concern for the health of the children's bodies, she was forgetting their souls.

Pearl Buck's biography of her mother builds up a total and well-rounded portrait of a many-faceted woman, who, in so many ways, led an unhappy and frustrating existence. Pearl Buck once complimented Ida Tarbell on her autobiography because, in particular, Tarbell had put her heart and soul into the book; and this quality, Buck believes, forms the essence of a good biography.[12] This feature is definitely pronounced in *The Exile*. Caroline Sydenstricker's heart and soul are enclosed within the pages of this book, and one could not conceive of a more pentrating insight.

Her daughter believes that if Caroline could have looked back at her whole life, she would have regarded it as a failure, primarily because her search for beauty and spiritual fulfillment was never realized. But perhaps, she thinks, her mother's spirit could never be fulfilled because it was a mixture of the practical and the mystical, of the skeptic and of the religious believer.[13]

While *The Exile* is an amazingly and genuinely frank and complete picture of a missionary wife, it is not without fault. At times the biography becomes too sentimental, and this quality comes to the fore particularly in the treatment of Caroline Sydenstricker's youth in West Virginia, her love for her home and family, and her continued devotion to and longing for America. When Pearl is married and when Caroline's beloved brother Cornelius dies, for example, not only does the thought dwell too much on the emotions involved, but the style itself becomes a bit too flowery, too tender, too romantic for modern taste. Further, *The Exile* is at times too diffuse and repetitive; on occasion it needs to be tightened, to be fixed more firmly on the main materials. But, with all these obvious weaknesses, the portrait drawn of Caroline Sydenstricker remains imprinted in one's memory; and the character analysis is rendered with persuasive depth. The reader not only sees the principal external events of her life, but, more importantly, is taken into her mind and being and brought to a convincing understanding of her aspirations, her temptations, her spiritual turmoil, her sorrows, and her frustrations.

II   Fighting Angel

If *The Exile* is a fine biography, *Fighting Angel* (despite an old-fashioned ring its title) is an even better one. While *The Exile* is on occasion too wordy and too repetitive, *Fighting Angel* is much more taut and focused. Now and then *The Exile* becomes sentimental because Buck admired her mother deeply and was exceptionally devoted to her. Toward her father, however, she is less sympathetic and more objective; hence, the portrait of Absalom Sydenstricker unfolds in a harsher, rougher fashion. That this treatment resulted in a more effective biography can be seen from a comparison between *Fighting Angel* and "In Memoriam: Absalom Sydenstricker, 1852–1931," a biographical sketch written shortly after Absalom's death in 1931.[14]

"In Memoriam" is primarily a factual account of Absalom Sydenstricker's life; it is a eulogy stressing only his positive accomplishments: his pioneering work in establishing the Presbyterian mission in North China, his work in founding native seminaries, his translation of the New Testament into Chinese. These and other achievements are recorded in a straightforward, sympathetic manner. So sympathetic is the approach in the "In Memoriam" essay that it contrasts sharply with the more objective, balanced account in *Fighting Angel*, which in sheer character portrayal and in totality of analysis is a fascinating study.

Absalom Sydenstricker was one of seven sons of a domineering West Virginia farmer, six of whom became ministers. All the sons had to work on the land until they were twenty-one; then they were free to work out their own destiny. At the age of manumission Absalom left his father's farm to enroll at Frankfort Academy. After a year there he entered Washington and Lee University. During his college years he was frightfully poor, but he loved school with an abiding passion and graduated with honors. After a time he entered a Presbyterian seminary to become a missionary. His father opposed his desire, but his mother concurred, providing he could find a wife to go to China with him. Absalom was extremely shy and not at all interested in girls; yet his meeting with Caroline Stulting gave him the opportunity to achieve his goal. In many ways the wife his mother required him to have was only a convenience, someone whom he often forgot, someone whom he regarded as only a background figure. When it came time to leave after their marriage, Absalom absentmindedly bought only one ticket for the train trip.

Yet from the time Absalom and his wife set out for China, he was serenely happy and content because he was dedicated to his religious vocation and was performing the work he loved. When he and Caroline arrived in China, they studied the Chinese language eight hours a day, six days a week. Caroline often grew weary and restless. When asked if he felt bored from such an intense effort, Absalom responded, "How could I be tired when I was doing the one thing I most wanted to do—fit myself for the Work?"[15]

Everything else—even the welfare of the members of his own family—was ruthlessly sacrificed to his missionary zeal. He constantly traveled on long missionary journeys. His usual procedure was to visit a town or village, sit in a tea shop, and wait for a crowd to gather. He would tell the gathering he was from America, inquire about their community, and begin to preach. He would give out or sell religious tracts, and then leave. Some time later he would return; again a crowd would gather, and he would preach. This pattern was repeated; a room facing the street would be rented, a few benches procured, and a chapel set up for services. When a few converts were gained, the same procedure was repeated in additional villages, while a more experienced convert from another community was placed in charge of the new chapel. Absalom would then revisit the new chapels twice a year and perform the necessary religious duties.

The converts themselves were a varied lot: old women searching for some kind of inner peace, people seeking work, or desiring to learn English and obtain a job in some large city, or people believing that all gods are beneficial, or people who were caught by the zeal of the preacher.

Often Absalom was received with hostility. He was beaten, robbed, stoned, and cursed. Once he awoke from sleep to find a man standing over him with a meat-chopper. Absalom prayed aloud, and the strange English words frightened the assassin. When the assassin asked Absalom what he was saying, Absalom told him that he was praying to his God and that, if the man killed him, the assassin would live on in suffering. The would-be killer grew frightened and withdrew. During the Boxer Rebellion and the Revolution of 1926–27 Absalom again barely escaped with his life. During the Boxer Rebellion Absalom was the only white man in his region; however, he was absolutely fearless while performing his missionary duties.

While his religious activities were, for the most part, highly successful, his family life was anything but ideal. He did not really understand his wife, for in temperament they were complete opposites. Absalom could not reach his children, and he refused to play with them as Caroline did. He was a stranger to his offspring; so much so that his daughter could look back at her birth and remark that "it was entirely insignificant because it made no difference to Andrew."[16]

When a young schoolgirl, Pearl remembers showing her report card to her father on a particular occasion when her mark in geometry was 99; his comment was, "A good mark, a hundred would have been better."[17] During her childhood Pearl Buck disliked her father, and it is not difficult to see why. Absalom Sydenstricker was so interested in his religious mission that he did not regard his children with especial warmth. Later on, when he became senile and she came to take care of him, her attachment for him grew, and she appreciated him fully. In addition to the "In Memoriam" tribute, she has written of her father most affectionately in *My Several Worlds*.[18] But the most forceful impressions in *Fighting Angel* are those of her childhood and relatively early experiences.

Absalom's children were always far secondary to his work, and his children realized this and resented it. Although he was an effective missionary and father to countless Chinese, he was not in fact a father to his own children. His sons and daughters "were bereaved in what they never had, in what he could not give them, because he had given everything in him to God."[19] Absalom could not make his religion and his inherent goodness vital to his children. He was too stern, too forbidding, too rigid, too unsympathetic.

All his life he was alone. Even as a boy in the bosom of his family, he felt shy and different. At no time in his life did he have a close friend—nor did he attempt to achieve any emotional or intellectual companionship with his wife. He lived within himself, completely unconcerned about people's opinions. He listened to and communed with God alone and never doubted that his ways were God's ways. He never doubted his mission. Stephen Vincent Benét and Rosemary Benét liken him, with much justice, to a modern St. Paul.[20]

Besides a vividly realized portrait of a human being, there emerges from *Fighting Angel* a compelling delineation of the nineteenth-century type of crusader—the essence of rock-ribbed individualism, a fiery zeal which, depending upon the direction in which it was channeled, could produce a General Charles Gordon, a John D. Rockefeller, a David Livingstone. Pearl Buck sees her father as a manifestation of a spirit that especially permeated America at a particular time. She comments that this spirit was based on a fervor and zeal of purpose with an unshaken confidence in the right of what was being done. She can write with candor and truth:

I have not seen anyone the like of [Absalom] and his generation. They were no mild stay-at-homes, no soft-living landsmen. If they had not gone as daring missionaries, they would have gone to gold fields or explored the poles or sailed on pirate ships. They would have ruled the natives of foreign lands in other ways of power if God had not caught their souls so young. They were proud and quarrelsome and brave and intolerant and passionate. There was not a meek man among them. They strode along the Chinese streets secure in their right to go about their business. No question ever assailed them, no doubt ever weakened them. They were right in all they did and they waged the wars of God, sure of victory.[21]

Pearl Buck sees the faults as well as the values of these men. And this balance of viewpoint makes Henry Seidel Canby's observation authoritative: "Her biographies of her parents are unquestionably the best studies ever done of the unique personal traits developed by the missionary fervor of the nineteenth century, which, some day, will be recognized as a very important part of the social history of Western civilization in that departed epoch."[22]

In addition to the individual portrait, Pearl Buck graphically depicts missionary life in China, particularly in a closely knit missionary community. Many of these people, obliged to live and work together in proximity, had no liking for one another. Often they would find no relief in what they regarded as the alien civilization about them; so they not infrequently became unhappy and warped and, thereby, complicated the problems of missionary existence. Several cases are cited, such as that of a gentle married missionary who eventually went insane because of his guilt in taking a Chinese concubine. Another missionary was periodically subject to fits, during which he believed his wife was unfaithful; and he would, accordingly, attempt to kill her. Then there were the lonely missionary spinsters, some of whom became stern and unfeeling tyrants; others, gentle and saintly. These and similar materials reverberate throughout *Fighting Angel*, and the realism and vividness of the work sear into the mind of the reader.

Aside from the elimination of some repetitiousness of idea here and there, perhaps the only way *Fighting Angel* could have been improved would have been to include more instances of Absalom's experiences on his long missionary journeys. There is a sketchiness about Absalom's field activities, obviously because he was often too taciturn and too humble to discuss them.

Fighting Angel is written in an extremely simple style, which is justified and effective on two counts. First, Pearl Buck mixes childhood memories with later knowledge of her father, and the plain narration of biographical events enhances the effect of the impressions made by a father on his daughter. Second, the simple word choice sharply focuses on and points up the picture of the main character. The simplicity of the prose makes the portrait stark and more penetrating and results in a concentration that is throuthly revealing.

Both *The Exile* and *Fighting Angel* are decidedly superior biographies. The influence these books exercised on the Nobel Prize Committee becomes quite easy to understand. Both works are neglected at the present time because of the decline of Pearl Buck's literary reputation. One feels, however, that they will be rediscovered and treasured, not only as examples of excellent biographical writing but also as pictures of two completely rendered Americans and of a historical phenomenon characteristic of a particular time and place.

CHAPTER 5

The Nobel Aura

U P to this point in her career Pearl Buck had confined her creative writing to Chinese subjects. More and more, however, she was familiarizing herself with American scenes and life. In 1932 Chinese governmental instability, the Communist menace, the Japanese attack on Manchuria, Japan's continued aggressive actions, plus anti-foreign feeling convinced her that white people would eventually be driven from China. Her invalid child was being cared for in the United States, and Pearl Buck felt a deepening need to be near her as much as possible.

Her marriage to John Lossing Buck had not been particularly happy, and the couple decided to separate.[1] In 1934 she left China to settle permanently in the United States. The following year she was divorced from her first husband and married Richard J. Walsh, the president of the John Day publishing firm. Before her second marriage she had purchased a home in Bucks County, Pennsylvania; there she settled in as an American wife determined to continue her writing career. The first detailed manifestation of her new interest in American subject matter was a novel entitled *Now and Forever* written for magazine serialization.[2] This work—slight, slick, and frivolous—was followed in 1938 by the publication of another novel of the American scene, a novel of more serious proportions.

I This Proud Heart

This Proud Heart is a study of the life and character of Susan Gaylord. Susan possesses a tremendous amount of vitality. She is extremely intelligent, enthusiastic, and does everything from housework to piano playing with exceptional facility. Teachers, friends, and her own family notice and remark that she is very "different" from the average person.

Susan wants to experience everything she can. Nothing—her

parents, her husband, her children, her career as a sculptress—seems to be enough for her satisfaction. She evinces a gusto for life and for complete fulfillment equal to that which is associated most commonly in the reader's mind with Thomas Wolfe and his protagonists. Her husband feels inadequate to her needs; and, although she loves him, she cannot completely convince him of his importance to her. The famous sculptor David Barnes, who realizes that Susan has the gift of genius, is alternately attracted to and repelled by her. Barnes is furious that a woman has been given such a magnificent talent; yet he urges her to study in Paris. She refuses to leave her household duties, although her natural talent needs development by further training. While sculpturing, Susan loses herself completely in the exhilaration of creation; nevertheless, she remains unwilling to give up everything in a single-minded pursuit of artistic perfection. In her autobiographical testament *A Bridge for Passing*, Pearl Buck remarks of herself: "I am divided to the bottom of my being, part of me being woman, the other part artist and having nothing to do with woman."[3] This comment exactly fits Susan, torn between her feminine emotional needs plus her desire to live life to the fullest, and her necessity for artistic satisfaction.

Through an obvious plot manipulation, Susan's husband dies. Freed from some family responsibility, she takes her children and travels to France to study. She works both in clay and in marble, but she comes to prefer the latter. In Paris, Susan devotes herself to her work, and she is now able to acknowledge that she is "different." She understands that she would have eventually gone to Europe, even if it had meant breaking up the marriage. But she is still not ready to accept David Barnes's dictum that, for a genuine artist, nothing counts but work. Barnes had formerly allowed various women to distract him, but now he is single-mindedly dedicated to his career. Susan's emotional nature, however, still requires nourishment.

She meets Blake Kinnaird, a wealthy American modernist artist, and marries him. They return to the United States. For a year Susan directs her full attention to Blake, but she starts to realize that he is stifling her creative desires. She begins to sculpture but learns that Blake is jealous of her work. When she discovers that he is involved in a love affair, she is further disillusioned. The death of Susan's father, a poet and college professor who has been frustrated by his wife's narrowness and sense of convention, brings her to a complete awareness of her need to fulfill herself through art alone. She and Blake separate, and she can now devote herself, with undivided attention, to creation.

Thematically, *This Proud Heart* is most interesting. The problem of a woman genius—a woman who has both an excellent mind and natural creative talent—who at the same time is desirous of love, motherhood, and normal family life is posed with feeling and realism. Autobiographical material is at work here. Indeed, when William Lyon Phelps asked Buck if she herself was Susan, her reply was "I don't know—perhaps—a little!"[4] Theodore Harris, Buck's official biographer, leaves no doubt that much of the material is based on personal, real-life experiences.[5]

While treatment of the male genius is not especially uncommon in writing, *This Proud Heart* is one of the few mature attempts in fiction to explain and study a woman genius. It is true that Pearl Buck is never able to explain satisfactorily Susan Gaylord's uniqueness. Susan's almost inexhaustible energy is apparent, and the reader feels the waves of desire to create that frequently swell through her being. Several reviewers of this novel complained that the reader does not come to understand the reasons for Susan's genius. But understanding genius is really an impossibility, and it must be acknowledged that the author has presented Susan's characteristics on a credible level and that the conflict between her artistic drives and her romantic needs is sharply defined. Yet Susan is not a completely satisfying creation, principally because Buck's viewing-on-the-outside method of storytelling does not enable us to get deeply enough inside her mind. The author tells of Susan's genius, and it is acknowledged by Barnes and by her French *maître*. The differences she possesses are also commented upon by most of the characters who come in contact with her. And yet, with all of this data to help us, we do not really become convinced by Susan: she is too often aloof and remote from the reader. While external narration may be effective in saga-like chronicles or in biographies, it does not go far enough or deep enough to help us understand Susan's genius more completely and to render her an unforgettable character. A more mental technique of intro-spection, such as the stream-of-consciousness method, appears necessary in order to bring the problem of genius to a more thorough visualization. The novel is also not helped by surrounding Susan with a handful of stock and type characters. While they never quite succeed in dragging her down to their level, they do dull her luster and weaken our appreciation of her uniqueness.

While the thematic problem posed in *This Proud Heart* intrigues, and the explanation of the problem carries us to about as satisfactory a solution as possible, the novel loses considerable impact because of its stylistic weaknesses. Coming from a reading of the Chinese novels, from a reading of *The Exile* and *Fighting Angel*, one notices immediately the lack of poetic beauty, the lack of exquisite descriptions, and the pedestrian nature of the writing. Many of the phrases are nothing but clichés. Phrases such as "cold heart," "living kindness," "her heart pounding," "chill of autumn," "her heart leaped up in her breast," "glistening black," and "bitterness of the north wind" abound. Certain words are reiterated again and again. For example, the word "passionate" in its noun, adjective, and adverbial forms appears over twenty-five times in the course of the book, four times on the first eight pages. The word "beautiful" is used almost fifty times so that descriptions such as "beautiful old house," "beautiful pose," "beautiful home" seem almost ubiquitous. The word choice is exceedingly simple, and Buck's selection of nouns and adjectives lacks both variety and a sense of freshness. Further, the dialogue is frequently stiff, forced, and stilted. So ordinary and flat is the style and mechanics of presentation that the overall effect of the novel is reduced.

This Proud Heart still arouses interest, but this is based on the purely intellectual problem of an artistic talent in a workaday world. What is especially evident in this novel is the hard core of mental activity in Pearl Buck's work which continually helps to elevate it above the superficiality of ordinary best sellers. In her fiction she usually presents some theme with which the reader can wrestle intellectually. Even if the book does not succeed, one feels that he is in the company of an alert and challenging mind which offers much valuable thought and insight. Stylistically, *This Proud Heart* is a disaster; thematically, it has several rewarding moments.

II *The Awarding of the Nobel Prize*

When the Nobel Prize Committee sat down to consider their choice, they had nine of Pearl Buck's books to work with: *East Wind: West Wind*, the *House of Earth* trilogy, *The Mother*, the two biographies, a short and unimportant novel on the missionary movement,[6] and *This Proud Heart*. That the main factors in the judgment of the committee were the novels on Chinese life and the biographies of Buck's father and mother has previously been noted. Anders Osterling, Permanent Secretary of the Swedish Academy and Chairman of the Nobel Committee on Literature, wrote:

The decisive factor in the Academy's judgment was, above all, the admirable biographies of her parents, the missionary pair in China—two volumes which seemed to deserve classic rank and to possess the required prospects for permanent interest. In addition, her novels of Chinese peasant life have properly made a place for themselves by virtue of the authenticity, wealth of detail and rare insight with which they describe a region that is little known and rarely accessible to Western readers. But as literary works of art the two biographies remain incomparable with anything else in Pearl Buck's both earlier or later production.[7]

Needless to remark, considerable criticism about giving the Nobel award to Buck took place. Just as more recently, when the prize was presented to John Steinbeck, much surprise, outrage, and dissent occurred.

In order to understand the Nobel Committee's judgment, several factors must be noted. First of all, the award was not primarily a "political" prize, as has been maintained by some critics. The fact that Pearl Buck's writing exemplified a "one-world" humanitarian sympathy, while it unquestionably increased Buck's reading audience, does not appear to have swayed the award committee to any appreciable extent.

Second, Pearl Buck's writings have been immensely popular abroad. In Spiller's *Literary History of the United States* it is recorded that her work was "particularly liked in Sweden. Ten of her books appeared there between 1932 and 1940, more than were translated from any other American author during the years covered by the *Index Translationum*."[8] It is further stated that in Denmark she "was the most popular American author from 1932 to 1939 . . . but Hemingway and Steinbeck had succeeded her by 1940."[9] What was generally true in Sweden and Denmark held for much of the world.[10] Eventually, Pearl Buck's writings were translated into every important language in the world. She and Mark Twain have become unrivaled among American writers—both past and present—for their top-ranking place of popularity in countries overseas. The impact of an American writer on foreign countries is always a fundamental factor that influences the Nobel Committee's judgment—a fact often forgotten or deliberately ignored by American literary critics. On the basis of her foreign impact alone, Pearl Buck would be high on a list of considered authors.

Too often today, Buck is judged on the basis of her work after receiving the Nobel Prize. While it has become a critical commonplace to remark that a writer's best work is always completed before the Nobel Prize is granted (the reward itself seeming always to mark a decline in the writer's talent), this situation is particularly true of Pearl Buck's efforts. In the 1930s she produced several fine books; after this decade she never again reached the same level of achievement.

Buck acknowledges the blow she suffered when so many of her fellow American writers attacked her for receiving the Nobel Prize. It was claimed that she was too youthful, that she had written too few important books to be considered of major stature, and that no woman writer deserved the award. She was even charged with not being an American writer since her subject matter and even her places of residence were almost completely Chinese. When she was honored at a dinner in New York City, she was filled with a deep sense of depression at such recent attacks. Remembering the Chinese belief that a storyteller is not accepted as a significant author, she gave as part of her speech some of the preface of *Shui Hu Chuan*, which made an apologetic commentary on novel writing, regarding it as inferior to more scholarly composition.[11] Her reception by American creative writers was not calculated to give her confidence in her work and to increase in her mind the stature of novel writing.

A few creative authors demurred from the general attitude toward Pearl Buck's award. The most important of these was Sinclair Lewis. At a banquet he complimented Buck for having "given a new picture of the Orient in terms of human beings."[12] Privately, he told her not to underestimate her powers and not to demean the novel as an art form.[13] Unfortunately, however, Buck, as she herself acknowledges, did not grow up in an environment that was conducive toward an artistic view of the novel.

While deciding, before the age of ten, on a career as a writer of novels, the youthful author was distressed by the attitude and theories of her Confucian tutor, Mr. Kung. Kung was educated in the classical tradition in China which did not regard novels highly. Confucius objected to novels because, he alleged, they induced immorality and turned men away from philosophy. Novels were considered nothing but entertainment and were, therefore, not looked upon as genuine literature. Since the state examinations for important positions were given in classical Chinese writing, scholars had a pragmatic excuse for ignoring the traditional saga-like story.[14] This attitude of the Chinese intellectuals, together with her parents' religious feelings that novel reading or writing was not a serious endeavor, admittedly lowered her regard for the novel as a work of art.[15]

While the Nobel award to Pearl Buck produced many scoffers and detractors, several literary critics came to her defense. Henry Seidel Canby, writing in the *Saturday Review of Literature*, assumed that Buck had received the prize for *The Good Earth*: "they [the Nobel Committee] are, they must be crowning one book, a masterpiece which richly deserves exalted recognition . . . a unique book, and in all probability belongs among the permanent contributions to world literature of our times."[16] Canby felt that the award to Buck was justified and that *The Good Earth* had proved its greatness around the world.

Malcolm Cowley, writing in the *New Republic*, noted that *The Good Earth* "continues to be jeered at or neglected" in American literary circles since it "didn't succeed in the fashion that critics regard as orthodox."[17] That is, the critics did not first discover *The Good Earth* and then spread its reputation until it was picked up by the general public. Cowley maintained that the critics were offended because the public had, so to speak, stolen a march on them:

[Pearl Buck] was discovered by the public at large while the literary scouts were looking the other way. I know that "The Good Earth" was extravagantly praised by pundits like William Lyon Phelps, but the effect in serious literary circles was merely to clinch the case against her.

On reading "The Good Earth" after all these years, I found that Mr. Phelps was right for once, and the highbrow critics mistaken. Mr. Phelps was the first, I think, to call the book a masterpiece. . . . If we define a masterpiece as a novel that is living, complete, sustained, but still somewhat limited in its scope as compared with the greatest works of fiction—if we define it as "Wuthering Heights" rather than "War and Peace"—then Mr. Phelps has found exactly the word for "The Good Earth."[18]

Oscar Cargill discussed Buck's Nobel award in the following manner: "To reflective Americans outside the [literary] fraternity, to the 'barbs' at least, the prize seemed well given as a reminder that pure aestheticism is not everything in letters. If the standard of her work was not so uniformly high as that of a few other craftsmen, what she wrote had universal appeal and a comprehensibility not too frequently matched."[19]

Just as her clarity and comprehensiveness in range appealed to Oscar Cargill, so too did these features attract the Nobel group. In particular, it was the universality of her view and the timelessness of her setting and tone that actually did much to recommend her books.

III   *Buck's Literary Theories*

The earliest expression of Pearl Buck's literary theories is found in two formative addresses, concerned mainly with the Chinese novel, which were delivered in Peiping in February, 1932.[20] In her analysis of the traditional Chinese story she notes that the author is omniscient, although the author's presence is not advertised. She finds that the Chinese novel contains relatively little description and what description there is, is largely external. Characters are revealed by action and by dialogue, and seldom does one find exposition of internal states of mind. In the course of her remarks, Buck does attack the Western behavioristic novel because it imposes a rigidity of viewpoint that condemns mankind to a narrow, mechanical, and one-sided type of existence.[21]

She records that intellectuals and Confucian scholars deplored the indigenous Chinese novel. Nevertheless, she emphasizes the popularity of these tales. She notes that professional storytellers wandered through the country and set up booths where the people could gather to listen. The narrator of the tale took up a collection to pay for his time and effort. The ordinary Chinese particularly enjoyed these yarns, just as they delighted in plays given in the open air by roving groups of actors. This love of story, of the working out of a plot, engrossed Chinese audiences; and it is evident that Miss Buck regards this element as of the utmost significance.

Buck's most complete discussion of literary theory occurs in her Alumnae Address "On the Writing of Novels" delivered at Randolph-Macon Woman's College in June 1933.[22] At the outset of the speech she declares her enjoyment in writing fiction, but she does not like rules for writing. She has often been asked if the characters in her novels are real people, and she finds such a question difficult to answer. Characters in her work are, on the one hand, more simple than real human beings and, on the other hand, more complex than humans. She simplifies individuals when turning them into fictional figures so that they will fit the atmosphere, theme, and total picture. Anything that does not agree with the overall features of the scene and the story must be suppressed. At the same time, the novelist adds his own touches and flourishes to the characters, making them more imaginative and more complex than they are in real life.

Buck states that she is more obsessed by characters than she is by a plot. Characters continually appear in her mind and call out to her to put them into a book. Such characters must be controlled and used to unify a book, although these individuals frequently want to dominate the author. The major characters direct the plot and shape it as it develops. Buck claims that she knows the whole story, even the ending, before she begins to write.

Discussing various forms of telling a story, Buck does not believe that one method is intrinsically better than another. The artist should choose the form that is most appropriate for his material. This is the only criterion that matters, and literary criticism that decrees otherwise Buck finds faulty. She insists that the modern techniques of novel writing are not superior to the older methods. The novelist who is interested more in form than in people, she argues, is not creative, only inventive. If the writer is obsessed with the story and the characters, then the story and characters develop the most suitable form for their revelation.

In regard to style, Buck chooses some words from Virginia Woolf as the best definition of this quality. Good style consists of the use of "the far side of language." Style should bring meaning and emotion which goes beyond the words themselves. She feels that the simplest words are often the most powerful in bringing about such evocative effects.

Buck admits that the didactic novel is now frowned upon by literary critics, and she herself acknowledges that the genuine artist should not be a preacher. She is, however, not satisfied with this condition. She asserts that a worthwhile novelist like Thornton Wilder teaches through his writings, and she is personally attracted to the moral value in didacticism. Art may be didactic, she declares, if it describes life completely and firmly; but only the greatest genius could so handle art, and such a writer would avoid didacticism because it would disturb artistic proportion. The moralizer can never be a genuine artist because the picture of life portrayed would be distorted in order to fit the preachment. Life should be the teacher, not the novelist. She recognizes that the true artist should observe and portray life as it is and not twist it to fit a particular theory.

Five years later when Buck traveled to Stockholm to receive the Nobel Prize, she gave her Nobel lecture on the Chinese novel.[23] In this pivotal address she explained the main influence on her work, as well as her philosophy of composition. She traces her origins as a writer to the traditional Chinese novel. According to Buck, the Chinese reader was interested in action and in the effectiveness of character portrayal which arose from dialogue and the character's behavior rather than from the author's analysis. The ordinary Chinese writer of novels, she declares, was not interested in technique; to the extent that he was concerned about technique, "he ceased to be a good novelist and became a literary technician."[24]

Special attention to style was not a primary consideration because such concern could distract from the narrative. Speaking of the style of the native Chinese saga, Pearl Buck remarks:

[the style] was one which flowed easily along, clearly and simply, in the short words which they themselves used every day, with no other technique than occasional bits of description, only enough to give vividness to a place or a person, and never enough to delay the story. Nothing must delay the story. Story was what they wanted.[25]

After much discussion of the indigenous Chinese novel, Buck came to the central part of her own literary credo. Since this pronouncement is so important for an understanding of her writing, it is quoted in full:

And like the Chinese novelist, I have been taught to want to write for these people [the ordinary man and woman]. If they are reading their magazines by the million, then I want my stories there rather than in magazines read only by a few. For story belongs to the people. They are sounder judges of it than anyone else, for their senses are unspoiled and their emotions are free. No, a novelist must not think of pure literature as his goal. He must not even know this field too well, because people, who are his material, are not there. He is a story teller in a village tent and by his stories he entices people into his tent. He need not raise his voice when a scholar passes. But he must beat all his drums when a band of poor pilgrims pass on their way up the mountain in search of gods. To them he must cry, "I, too, tell of gods!" And to farmers he must talk of their land, and to old men he must speak of peace, and to old women he must tell of their children and to young men and women he must speak of each other. He must be satisfied if the common people hear him gladly. At least, so I have been taught in China.[26]

This crucial declaration with all its implications sums up many of the strengths and weaknesses of Pearl Buck's writing and indicates her basic philosophy in regard to literary production. From her statements on the Chinese novel, one can understand the development of Buck's literary ideas and her allegiance to the doctrine of the storyteller. Yet one can also see the limitations of such a creed. As Lewis Gannett pointed out in a review of this speech when it was published in book form, such a doctrine would suggest that Zane

Grey, Harold Bell Wright, Edgar Rice Burroughs, and Gene Stratton Porter are the really significant American novelists.[27] Certainly Buck does not mean to suggest this; and barring several pot-boilers, her own fiction is on a more significant thematic plane.

In the light of her statements made in the Nobel Prize acceptance speech, Pearl Buck seems to have become convinced of the value of reaching the largest audience possible. More and more she wrote articles for magazines and began to dilute her creative efforts in the novel form with nonfiction studies, children's books, and humanitarian interests. She was criticized because of her desire to reach a mass audience. In answer, she asserted before the National Education Association: "One cannot dismiss lightly a magazine bought and read by three million people. . . . It is important. It is a serious thing for literature if three million people read—not literature, but something which gives them greater satisfaction."[28]

Such an attitude would obviously preclude future attempts at reaching a more aesthetic approach to the novel. Losing oneself in the lesser forms of writing, and turning to more ephemeral themes necessarily reduced time for contemplation, for revising and rewriting novels, and for careful reworking of creative materials in order to produce the most artistic effects. Again and again in Pearl Buck's post-Nobel Prize work, one can recognize that if more time had been taken for writing and rewriting and for probing for depth in character development, the finished products would be more truly artistic. Buck comes to a point of subordinating her natural talent and ability to a narrow and limited creed of composition and to what is often communication for mass propaganda purposes.

In her biography of Pearl Buck, Cornelia Spencer has noted Buck's growing desire to reach a mass audience and the importance she attached to this purpose. Cornelia Spencer approves of this development in no uncertain terms:

Underlying her interests and her writing and her other active life there was and there is one unchanging unity. . . . All she does must work toward mutual understanding between the common peoples of the earth and toward justice for all. Through her first books she interpreted China to the West. Now the base of her interpretation was enlarging and deepening to include common people everywhere. As the subject matter of her writing broadened so also must her audience. More and more, then, in keeping with her purpose she wrote where she would be read, not only by the student and lover of books but by the workman and the clerk and the stenographer. With deliberate intent she wrote that everyone might read because she wants to write for people.[29]

In addition to her adherence to the technique of the traditional Chinese novel, and her desire to reach the widest possible audience with her humanitarian interests, a third factor was apparently involved in Buck's decision not to devote herself as fully as possible to the novel as an artistic form. This third element concerned a constitutional or temperamental excess of energy, which had too much drive and too many interests to confine itself to the strict, exhausting discipline of the novel as an art form. On one occasion Pearl Buck told her sister: "My great fault is that I can never give myself entirely to any one thing. I always seem to be concerned in several interests and I just have to be that way. I could not possibly choose one. The trouble is that I always have too many things I am interested in and live too many lives."[30]

With all of these factors there exists perhaps, in part, a real-life counterpart of the Susan Gaylord dilemma witnessed in *This Proud Heart*, for Susan's genius was hampered by a wide variety of interests and her emotional and womanly needs. Finally, Susan isolates herself from distractions and devotes herself totally to art. Unlike the fictional Susan Gaylord, Buck did not make an ultimate dedicated choice of art.

IV   *Medieval and Gunpowder Women*

Buck's growing interest in nonfictional topics was reflected in the publication of a considerable number of articles produced by her in the latter part of the 1930s and in the early 1940s. While not a militant feminist, Buck was concerned about woman's role in the modern world, and she began to write about the difficulties and characteristics of American women. She did succeed in arousing much discussion when she issued two celebrated essays on the themes of America's medieval women and America's gunpowder women.[31]

Pearl Buck contended that American society tends to treat modern women as if they lived in the medieval period. A woman may receive a well-rounded and solid education, which increases her desires and potentialities; yet, these very desires are often frustrated by the practices and customs of our society, which does not really want women outside the home. Further, she argued, that if women do work outside their home, they can obtain only subsidiary jobs or positions, ones in which men are not interested. Buck maintained that such a situation involves a frightful contradiction and that women should be given an equal opportunity to make reasonable and sensible use of the education they have received. Thus America, as a whole, is in a medieval frame of mind about the role of women in present-day life. America tends to be hidebound to the tradition that woman's place is in the home. When a woman obtains a good education, it is difficult for her to fulfill herself in her chosen field, to develop herself to the highest extent because convention is opposed to her self-realization. As our society is presently constituted, few women could become surgeons or obtain top positions in such a field as banking. Buck points out that women themselves frequently support America's medieval tendencies. They would, for example, prefer a male to a woman surgeon. Also, average women are frequently jealous of those who achieve eminence in some field. Since they themselves fit into the traditional mold of subordination, they do not like to see other women break the pattern and obtain more prominence. Obviously Pearl Buck's comments were truer at the time they were written than they are today. She was far ahead of her time.

Both men and women are at fault in the persistence of medieval practices. The adolescence and boyishness of many American men are out of place on an adult level, and the flighty, superficial attitudes of many American women discourage attempts to break away from the medieval pattern. Nevertheless, men should come to a realization that some women are at present different from the average and that all women potentially could arrive at a more happy, contented, and balanced existence than is now the case. Pearl Buck was distressed to note that, with all the freedom the American woman possesses and with all the privileges she enjoys, she is too often bored, restless, frustrated, and unfulfilled.

Buck divides America's women into three groups. The first group consists of talented women, most of whom are in the sciences or the arts. These women, a small percentage of the total, are dedicated and intensely devoted to their profession or interests. The second group are the satisfied homemakers who are completely wrapped up in household duties and in child rearing. The first two groups, she believes, are relatively small in contrast to the total number of women in the United States. Both these groups are doing what they wish to do; and, since they are satisfied in their pursuits, they constitute a worthwhile sensible multitude.

The third category is by far the largest. This group is composed of

America's gunpowder women. Buck defines gunpowder women as those who "have surplus time, energy, and ability which they do not know how to use."[32] These women idle their lives away by doing little but playing cards, going to movies, and gossiping. Pearl Buck insists that one can find a tremendous resource of wasted power among them, for they often have excellent mental equipment, but they do not put it to constructive use. Many women who do not work or have heavy family responsibilities have much time and energy to use in some way. Buck would have this time utilized for community improvement and planning, for the development of better education, and for various altruistic and humanitarian undertakings. By participating wholeheartedly in such activities, these women would render their own lives more fruitful, and their towns and cities as well as the nation as a whole would profit.

If more women entered the professions and specialized in medicine, science, and in other fields, they could make excellent contributions to American life. Buck was distressed because the percentage of professional women is so small. She feels that women have a responsibility to do more for society than they are now doing. Too many American women are discontented, and this discontentment is "spiritual gunpowder of the fullest inflammability."[33] Many a woman in the United States is "idle because nothing is demanded or expected of her and yet unable to be happy because she is idle."[34] Women should accept the challenge of work and service and make use of their inactive or wasted resources. Gunpowder women offer great potentiality for America's further development, but they need to be prodded into a realization of this potential.

In addition to her medieval and gunpowder women essays, Pearl Buck has written on numerous other topics involving both the women of the United States and those of the world. One of her most deeply felt ideas is that women should take an active role in achieving a just and lasting peace throughout the universe. Women have, she feels, too often abrogated their responsibility to prevent war and have too meekly submitted to following the demands and whims of men. Buck herself has always been strongly opposed to war or to any sort of military force. She insists that many men want war since it presents them with an opportunity for some excitement and heroism. In wartime man can allow his hatreds to find expression; he can achieve a measure of irresponsibility without being held accountable for it; and he can give vent to all types of emotion. Too many men, she argues, are willing to accept war as inevitable and to adjust philosophically to it as a normal part of living. Therefore, while men take the predominant place in world affairs, wars are bound to recur: "Man by himself has not been able to make war obsolete, as it should be among civilized people."[35] With the proper influence of women in world affairs, Buck feels that the futility and foolishness of war would become apparent to men and strife would eventually come under control. If war is to cease, she believes that this situation will occur through the influence of women.[36]

She is less persuasive when she speaks about controlling the type of individual such as Hitler or Napoleon who is one of the main causes of war.[37] She urges that such atavistic types should be discovered early in the educational process and that psychiatrists should treat them. If the animalistic and antisocial characteristics and desires of sub-human types cannot be controlled, then such individuals should be confined to institutions capable of caring for them. This belief is carried over into several of Buck's novels, most notably in *Bright Procession*, but perhaps most memorably in *Dragon Seed* when Ling Tan reflects "that only a certain kind of man made war,"[38] and that, if these men could be isolated, world peace would become inevitable.

Buck is inclined to split mankind into two separate groups. The smallest group is animalistic and uncivilized; it consists of those who because of barbarism and undeveloped mental processes continually plunge the world into war. To discover and control this small group is, unfortunately, not so simple a matter as Buck thinks. Although she feels that women should—as mothers, teachers, social workers, etc.—play an important role in the attempts to seek out and contain atavistic human beings, she is not convincing about the ways and means of accomplishing such a desirable goal. The whole question is further oversimplified in a failure to emphasize good and bad within each and every individual. Buck is too inclined to divide the world into "good guys" and "bad guys," too ready to regard most people as upright and basically decent, with only an infinitesimal percentage of the earth's population considered evil.

Another interesting point of view which Pearl Buck takes in her writings on matters involving women concerns the necessity for a common education for men and women. She believes that education from grade school to college should always be coeducational, that boys and girls should be grouped on the basis of biological age, and that the two groups should be taught the same subjects. She maintains that such educational training would remove antagonism between men and women and bring both groups to a deeper and closer understanding of each other. From a common sharing of knowledge and experiences, American women would achieve a greater measure of equality, become less discontented, contribute ideas and benefits to our national life, and live in a more harmonious relationship with men. She visualizes American education "shaped toward mutual understanding and appreciation between men and women."[39]

Many of Pearl Buck's ideas on sociological problems and the relationship between men and women are admittedly derivative. She considers, for example, the matriarchal nature of American society and the now-famous problem of "momism." She also directs attention to the well-known modern dilemma, which is not confined to suburbanites, of the father who sees very little of his children and does not spend enough time at home.

Several of her ideas are fresh and stimulating. She does, for example, make some arresting comparisons between American and Chinese practices. Noting the traditional Chinese pre-World War II stresses on family life, she asserts that the Chinese young man is encouraged to marry young, to bring his wife to live in his parents' home, and then to work or complete his education. If he should lose a position, he is aided by his family until he finds a new job. When his parents reach old age, it is his duty to take care of them; and, when he ages, his children are obligated to render the final years of his life secure. A cycle of loyalty and support marked the old Chinese family pattern.

In contrast, the American system often leads to problems which seem difficult to resolve. Since young men are often not financially able to marry when they should, Pearl Buck suggests more cooperation between generations based on the traditional Chinese model. Older people could help young people marry at an earlier age and help out in financial difficulties, while children could see that their parents received as much assistance as possible in their old age. She feels that this assistance must be rendered either by the family or by the state, and that the Chinese system appears to furnish more freedom for the individual.

Many of Pearl Buck's most provocative ideas on problems of human relationships, sociology, and related matters have circulated widely, and her basic ideas have been collected in a volume called *Of Men and Women* (1941). In 1962 she was asked if over twenty years later she would have written the same book. She answered she would keep *Of Men and Women* essentially the same, but that she would add a new development.[40] This new aspect would treat of men's growing respect for women since World War II. She finds that men have come to a greater awareness of woman's intelligence and of her ability in work. Men no longer want to restrict women to the home. Men, she believes, have come to seek more companionship from women on an intellectual basis; and, further, men are coming to a realization that they should and can work together with women to improve many aspects of life.

In 1971 *Of Men and Women* was reissued with a new epilogue entitled "Women and 'Liberation.'" Pearl Buck emphasizes here that the "gunpowder" women have begun to explode and that now women are more united and less jealous of one another. She asserts that men and women are now considering people not by sexual stereotypes but on the basis of individual strengths and weaknesses. She feels this new outlook will bring an equality among the sexes, which she supports in every way. She does caution about children, however, since if the parents do not assume familial responsibility, then the state will take over with the concomitant dangers observed in China under the regime of Mao Tse-tung.[41]

CHAPTER 6

Popular Novels and the War Crusade

THE late 1930s and the early 1940s represent an extremely success-ful period in Pearl Buck's career. Her writing and crusading work continued at a breakneck pace, and she attracted even wider audiences. Although she never lacked incredible energy, she seemed to receive fresh strength and incentive from the Nobel award and became even more active and productive.

I The Patriot

That Pearl Buck's decline as a novelist was not immediate and that she still could write novels worth attention and discussion was proved by the publication in 1939 of *The Patriot*. This narrative, Buck's first novel after receiving the Nobel Prize, considers the revolutionary movement in Shanghai in the late 1920s, Chiang Kai-shek's arrival, the immediate imprisonment and persecution of the National Brotherhood of Patriots, the Kuomintang's alliance with the moneyed classes, and the later Sino-Japanese War.

I-wan, the novel's principal male character, is a university student and the son of a Shanghai bank president. Coming under the influence of a young revolutionist named En-lan, I-wan becomes a student leader in the patriot movement, one of many young men who dreamed "of overthrowing the new republic and setting up a still newer one."[1] Chiang Kai-shek's recently established government is consolidating its position in Hankow, and these students regard Chiang as their hero. They believe their function is to prepare the way for Chiang's coming to Shanghai. Chiang's movement will sup-posedly abolish poverty and bring about superior living and working conditions. With En-lan and other members of the student league, I-wan works to indoctrinate the Shanghai silk mill workers so that they will support Chiang. A general strike occurs. Chiang sweeps down the Yangtse River, and both the young intellectuals and the poor await his arrival. Chiang, however, compromises with the Shanghai bankers, and the glorious dreams of freedom and improvement are shattered. The status quo is maintained. I-wan, En-lan, and the other student revolutionists are marked for execution as Communists. Nevertheless, I-wan manages to escape to Japan because of his father's financial power and influence.

I-wan goes to work for a Japanese import-export company and in time marries a Japanese girl. He is thoroughly disillusioned with Chiang Kai-shek and the failure of the revolution, and he does not wish to take further interest in world affairs. The Japanese carry on military attacks against the mainland, and the heavily censored Japanese newspapers give only limited and one-sided versions of events in Manchuria and China. According to news propaganda, the Chinese for the most part welcome the invaders, and the Japanese use force only against die-hards and militarists. From his wife's brother, who has returned from fighting in China, I-wan learns of Japanese atrocities, and the continued distortion in Japanese newspapers further intensifies his emotions. When I-wan's own brother visits him briefly, I-wan learns that a full-scale war between Japan and China is about to begin. Influenced by patriotism and duty, I-wan returns to his homeland to fight for China. Upon his return he witnesses an agreement between Chiang Kai-shek's Nationalists and the Chinese Communists, who had been driven into the northwestern part of the country. The Nationalists and the Communists are to unite in a struggle against their common enemy—Japan. This union, however, is unable to prevent one Japanese victory after another. Chiang's forces are pushed farther and farther inland, and only the Communists with their guerrilla tactics achieve some success. City after city falls to the Japanese, and at the end of the novel I-wan hears of the new Burma Road.

The Patriot possesses considerable value for its insights and explanations of relatively recent Chinese history, so that it furnishes a historical account of political and social importance. The narrative gives an excellent account of the hopes and techniques of the National Brotherhood of Patriots, an accurate picture of Shanghai before Chiang Kai-shek's arrival there, Chiang's opportunist and rightist tendencies, differing viewpoints on Japan's attacks on Manchuria and China as seen from both sides, the problem of the Kuomintang-Communist alliance against Japan, and the underlying differences between the two groups.

Part Two of the novel, which deals with I-wan's stay in Japan, is by far the most effective section. It presents one of the most realistic and convincing portraits of the Japanese character found in literature. Japanese attitudes of love of country, duty, and endurance are particularly well delineated; and Japanese qualities of delicacy, mannerliness, and love of beauty contrast sharply with their stoicism, militarism, and cruelty. The Japanese receive sorrow and catastrophe with amazing discipline. Notable in the novel is a marvelously striking scene of Japanese parents receiving the boxes of ashes of their sons who died in China. The portrait of one old man who smiles and yet cries at the same time, rejoicing that his only son has died for his country, is unforgettable.

Aspects of Japanese life and conduct in the period from 1928 to 1938 which are expertly captured are the slantings and distortions by news media, the persistent looting of Chinese heirlooms and treasures and their shipment to Japan, the dominance of the militarists, and the devotion of the people to this martial clique bound closely to Emperor worship. If the Japanese girl whom I-wan loves thought that a full-scale war between China and Japan would take place, she would have unhesitatingly married a widowed general, simply because of her duty to produce sons for her country's wars. In wartime, Tama Muraki asserts, "I would not have belonged to myself, but to my country."[2]

I-wan's consciousness of the many differences between the Japanese and Chinese are indicated particularly in his marriage to a Japanese girl. I-wan and Tama are foreign to each other in blood, in appearance, and in customs. They think differently about many things; yet I-wan comes to understand Tama's sense of duty, and Tama immediately understands the necessity for I-wan to return to fight for China. This necessity is the one thing about I-wan that Tama can comprehend and appreciate.

The novel also presents a searing picture of defective leadership in both countries. One senses the impressiveness of Chiang Kai-shek's bearing and his ability to dominate and to inspire his followers. At the same time, he is shown to be an opportunist and a chameleon of many colors. He can betray the revolutionary cause, and he can offer a bribe and execute the man who takes the money. When I-wan tasks his banker father with the news that Chiang has become a Christian and must, therefore, be untrustworthy, Wu the banker responds with the first joke his son has ever heard him utter: "He is doubtless using the Christians' God, too. . . . He is such a man."[3]

On the other hand, En-lan, who escapes Chiang's student purge and becomes a Communist leader, is primarily interested in fighting and in achieving power. Callous and thoroughly ruthless, he is just as anxious to regiment the poor as the rich. I-wan comes to believe that En-lan's honest simplicity is not comprehensive or enlightened enough to rule China in the long run. Neither Chiang nor the Communists can satisfy China's ultimate needs. Both may attempt to unite against Japan, but after the war neither side can furnish the leadership of justice and vision that China needs. On the other hand, Japan's leadership is anything but principled and sensible. Both participants in the Sino-Japanese War are impeded by inadequate, narrow rulers.

While En-lan is a fairly well rounded character and while the description of the Japanese temper and life is excellent, the character of I-wan does not at times convince us. Particularly in the first of the novel's three parts, we do not get deep enough inside I-wan to be convinced of his revolutionary goals and ideals and his willingness to let his own family be put to death. One is aware of too much authorial intrusion at this point rather than permitting the character to evolve through the action. In the remaining part of the novel I-wan's character is convincing. His disillusionment with Chiang, his frame of mind while living in Japan, his subsequent decision to return to his homeland, and his analysis of Chiang's behavior and En-lan's character—these and similar elements are thought out logically and in depth.

In writing *The Patriot* Pearl Buck discarded the poetic, semi-biblical style found in the *House of Earth* trilogy. Simplicity of style is retained, but the prose contains no poetry and no melodic movement. Nevertheless, while the style is characterized only by its utter simplicity and its matter-of-factness, it is perfectly suitable to the story and fits harmoniously into the narrative movement. It often helps to add a compelling verisimilitude of setting, especially to the Shanghai scenes and to the Japanese episodes.

The third part of *The Patriot* is the least successful. This section relates I-wan's return to China, his contact with Chiang Kai-shek, and his ultimate life with En-lan's guerrilla forces. I-wan is first sent to En-lan as Chiang's personal representative. This is an obviously transparent narrative maneuver to bring Chiang himself into the action. Much of the story manipulation in this last unit of the novel is too apparent and farfetched. Chiang himself, for example, personally calls in I-wan from the remote provinces merely to inform him that his brother is dead. That I-wan's former bondmaid would turn up as

En-lan's wife is another bit of contrivance and noticeable rigging. *The Patriot* is a cracking good story. It is such a tale as a village storyteller would relate in order to captivate his listeners, but in its final section it suffers from just such liberties as a storyteller too concerned about suspense and tying up loose ends would seize.

II Other Gods

The novel *Other Gods* (1940), subtitled *An American Legend*, deals with an aspect of life in the United States, although some scenes are set in China, India, and Tibet. In this book Pearl Buck studies the phenomenon and ramifications of hero worship. Influenced by the Charles Lindbergh flight, and perhaps by the then even more recent Douglas "Wrong-way" Corrigan episode, Buck focuses attention on Bert Holm, a young American mechanic who climbs to the top of a lofty peak in the Himalayas and in so doing captures the public's fancy. Buck is equally interested in Kit Tallant, the girl who marries Holm after he achieves fame. In the portraits of the American hero and his intellectual, poetry-writing wife, it is possible to visualize a roman à clef. That this possibility is not lost on Buck is seen in the standard disclaimer (unusual for her) at the start of the book stating that both the story and the characters are imaginary.

Bert Holm accompanies a British meteorological expedition attempting to climb Mt. Therat in the Himalayas. Bert's function is to tend two special-type caterpillar trucks. When the expedition is within eight hundred feet of the top, it is forced to turn back because of illness. Bert, however, leaves the group and climbs to the top alone. His daring feat is reported by the news services, and the imagination of the American public is deeply stirred.

On his way back to the United States, Bert stops over in Peking. There he meets Kit Tallant, the daughter of a wealthy New York family. Kit's father is in Peking to represent a New York bank negotiating a loan to China. Kit is just getting over a love affair. In this condition she meets the widely publicized hero, who happens to be an Adonis in appearance. In an aura of loneliness, rebounding from a previous love, and caught by Bert's handsome ruggedness and hero image, Kit marries him in Peking after a whirlwind courtship which has lasted about a month.

Upon their return to America, Bert and Kit are caught in all the public attention reserved for a popular hero. The young people are hardly able to have a moment to themselves. At first Bert is very annoyed by all of the fuss and interruption attendant upon his fame. In order to combat Bert's attitude and to avoid possible damaging news items, Kit's father hires a public relations expert to watch over Bert's public image and to keep the Tallant name from taint. Roger Brame, the public relations counsel who explains the importance of keeping Bert's reputation on a high level, insists that Bert has an obligation to conform to his public image; he, therefore, is not at liberty to do whatever he likes. The American people regard him as fearless, respectable, and thoroughly reliable. This view, Brame argues, should not be disturbed because a resultant negative reaction against Bert would be bitter and merciless.

As Kit comes to know her husband, she realizes that he is completely unintellectual, a naïve innocent with very little brainpower or imagination. Bert's silences are not the result of strength, reticence, or pensiveness; he simply has almost nothing to say because he thinks very little about anything. Kit, who is bright, sensitive, fastidious, and intense, comes to understand that Bert cannot give her intellectual or spiritual companionship. Bert is really an overgrown boy—physically attractive but limited in almost every other way. *Other Gods* contrasts continually the different way in which the public views its hero and the way his wife sees him. Kit is highly conscious of Bert's faults, but to the American newspaper reader, guided by Roger Brame's publicity handling, Bert is what a typical young American should aspire to be.

Failing to find the necessary comradeship with Bert which her spirit needs, Kit thinks more and more about her former lover. Realizing that a divorce would have a disastrous effect on Bert's reputation, Kit agrees to postpone a decision on this question until after a new expedition is organized to give Bert something to do and to keep him in the public eye. Moreover, Kit decides to accompany this expedition part of the way so that Bert's conduct in the Himalayas may somehow renew her faith in him and give her a legitimate reason for continuing their marriage.

When Bert nears the top of Mt. Pangbat, the goal of this latest expedition, he deserts his climbing partner so that he can reach the top first. Without leaving directions, he takes an alternate route and reaches the summit. As he looks down from the heights, Bert's view is obstructed by a cornice of snow. He pushes this pile of ice and snow and unintentionally starts an avalanche. Too late, he sees his climbing partner below, who is killed by the snow. Kit knows from Bert's conduct that in some way he has been instrumental in killing climber

Ronald Brugh. She threatens to leave him unless she is told what happened on the mountain. After his explanation, Kit realizes that Bert's selfishness and lack of thought were not premeditated. He was simply a child acting on impulses and hunches.

Upon their return to the States, Kit is faced with the decision to stay with or to divorce Bert. Bert is coming more and more to live according to his public image, although his inherent childishness always remains. As Kit ponders the public's reaction to Bert's second successful climb to the top of a Himalayan mountain, she reflects on what Bert means to the people. She decides that she cannot desert him; she cannot shatter the hopes, dreams, and wish-fulfillments of the public: "After all, dreams are all that most people have to live by," she said. "Out of mere duty, one can't—destroy them."[4]

In a prefatory note at the beginning of the novel, Pearl Buck states that she is fascinated with the problems faced by individuals who have been elevated by their fellowmen to a godlike status. She believes that a handful of such heroes "have been great enough to endure godhead; most of them have not. . . . They were made symbols and when they were compelled to this unearthly shape by that most powerful force on earth, the desire of men for a god, they were lost."[5]

Various aspects of hero worship are studied throughout the novel. The dangers of this tendency are noted in the rise of Hitler and Mussolini. It is a measure of Bert's immaturity and childishness that he thinks halfheartedly he might like to visit these two dictators just to see how they can control the people of their respective countries. Since Kit and Roger Brame labor under no misconceptions about this matter, Bert's half-articulated whim is not gratified. The dangers of hero worship are clearly apparent.

Other phases of the question of hero worship are probed. When a man is honored as an American hero, he is placed in a position for a mighty fall. If he disillusions his public, a violent reaction sets in against him. He is hated more vehemently because he was previously so completely worshiped. The shift from love to hate is drastic and frightening. Kit's father expresses the belief that Americans in particular must hate whatever they love because they do not really like to give up their own freedom and independence to anyone and because the old commandment against the worship of false gods is imbedded deep in their spirit. After a while the American comes to hate the other god. When Kit asks if Bert Holm is a false idol, her father's response is, "Any man is a false god to a people born of Puritans and Calvinists as we are, and nurtured on the Constitution. . . . And that's why if we love him, we are doomed to hate him."[6] The precarious nature of hero worship is well conveyed in *Other Gods*.

Two other manifestations of the problem of hero worship are interestingly noted. Roger Brame, the public relations counsel who does much to sustain Bert's image and to create it, comes to a need to believe in his own creation. Although he is fully cognizant of all Bert's faults and foibles, his spirit needs to believe in an ideal American type: the handsome young man of rural origins who stands for clean-cut, honorable living. It is a case of Pygmalion not only falling in love with his creation, but feeling deeply the spiritual need for such perfection.

The influence of hero worship on the hero himself is also indicated. Bert tells Kit near the end of the novel that he no longer gets drunk or flirts with women, that he wants to live up to the All-American type which the ordinary man envisions. And this comment is correct. Kit had often tried to alter such things as Bert's carelessness in appearance and his sulkiness. She could not effect such changes, but his public was able to bring about improvements by giving him adulation.

The various aspects of hero worship render the novel extremely satisfying on a problem-probing level. Unfortunately, the style does not achieve the level of the theme and the sensitive analysis of the topic discussed. But what might be called Buck's American style has improved. It is more mature, more elaborate, and more pliable than that of *This Proud Heart*. To be sure, it is still only journeyman prose, and the writing does not delight or scintillate as does her Chinese style. The novel is also weakened by some obvious manipulations intended to keep up suspense. For example, the presentation of Kit's former lover and of his desire to have her return is made unreal and artificial and is too consciously arranged to give Kit an alternate choice to life with Bert. The novel also has a peculiar bloodless quality, due partly to the style, but due also to an attempt to avoid the more realistic aspects of mob worship. It is only the problem studied in its various manifestations, the intellectual hard core of Pearl Buck's work, that raises the book above mere popular contrivance.

III   *Crusade during World War II*

The World War II years were busy ones for Pearl Buck. In addition to her creative work in fiction, she attempted to do everything possible to further the Allied war effort.[7] She made extensive use of radio in order to present plays that would enable the United States and China to exchange viewpoints and inspiration. Previously she had enrolled under an assumed name in a university radio script writing course. After studying radio writing techniques for several months, she authored several scripts. Among these efforts was *America Speaks to China*, a group of six radio plays written for the Office of War Information and broadcast to China by short wave. Other radio dramas such as *China to America* and *Will This Earth Hold?* presented ideas guaranteed to intensify America's support in China's struggle. Pearl Buck also wrote plays for United China Relief.[8]

In 1941 she was responsible for the founding of the East and West Association. This group attempted to bring both sides of the world to a closer understanding by studying characteristics of all nations and by seeking methods of harmonizing aims and goals. Buck carried on the work of this association throughout the war, handling particularly the educational material of the organization.[9]

Before and during America's entry into the war, Pearl Buck delivered numerous speeches and published articles, letters, and pamphlets intended to point up and clarify basic issues. Several of these productions received wide publicity and succeeded in making known points of view that had been mainly overlooked or forgotten in the furor of the time.

Perhaps Buck's most famous essay during the war period was "Tinder for Tomorrow," which appeared as an article, as a speech, and as an anthology selection.[10] This treatise considers the most recurrent and blatant theme of Japanese war propaganda: that the colored people of India, Malaya, the Philippines, and other countries in Southeast Asia cannot expect justice and fair treatment from America because of the white man's racial prejudices. Buck stresses that Chinese, Indian, and other people of Asia have often—both as individuals and as countries—been mistreated by white men, and that such abuse is remembered by the Asians. Japan's propaganda is, therefore, founded on a solid basis of experience. It seeks to ally all colored people of Asia against the white man, and produces a telling argument against supporting the United States by pointing to the condition of the blacks in America. Every race riot and every act of discrimination furnishes Japanese propaganda with effective grist, and the Japanese make full use of such material.

Buck emphasizes what is to become a recurring theme in her wartime addresses and publications: the people of Asia want freedom from colonial rule and from imperialism. This matter needs to be assessed and settled immediately, not put aside until the war is won. She asserts that the Asian peoples' patience with white supremacy and imperialism is at an end. She insists that the people of Asia know that, even if Germany and Japan are defeated, they themselves may have to fight later against the white men who are now their theoretical allies. In order to prevent this eventuality, to thwart Japanese propaganda, and to spur the colored people of Asia to greater fighting efforts, the United States at least should declare unequivocally that democracy and equality are not "to be limited to white people only."[11] Pearl Buck emphasizes the split personality of the average American: in theory he loves freedom and justice; in practice, he is filled with racial prejudice. She asserts that, if the United States is to persist in its present attitudes, it should logically join Hitler and fight on the side of fascism since racial prejudice is fascistic, not democratic. Fortunately, as in the case of the "women's movement," considerable improvement on racial issues has taken place since the 1940s.

In a variety of ways, in books, in magazine articles, in speeches, and on the radio, Buck continued her crusade during the war for total freedom for all people. In essays such as "What Are We Fighting For in the Orient?" and "Freedom for All,"[12] she proclaimed the necessity of insisting upon the end of colonialism and a declaration of equality everywhere; and she cautioned that future wars would result if this is not done.

As the war continued, Buck realized that the United States and Great Britain were unwilling to admit universal equality as a basic war aim. Thus, she noted a change in the initial drift of purpose. The war has not become a war for freedom; but—because of possessions held by such colonial powers as England, France, and Holland—it has simply become a war against the Axis powers. Thus, because there was no Western leader great and foresighted enough to declare "that this war was a war for the freedom of all peoples," we have "to face now . . . another war of which this one is only the beginning."[13] These particular words were spoken as early as December 10, 1942.

She notes that China is not being treated as an equal ally either in the planning of war strategy or in the supplying of weapons, particularly airplanes; and it is unlikely that China will be given an important position in later peace conferences. Even early in the war, plans had been made for European reconstruction and for providing food and medicine; but no plans had been created for relief of the starving in India or for medical aid in the Far Eastern countries. Instead of a war for human equality, our war goals have been frightfully narrowed: "It is now not even a war to save civilization. It is only a war to save European civilization."[14] Buck called upon the American people to speak out against this limitation. She maintained that the Four Freedoms do not include "the basic freedom—*the freedom to be free*."[15] Only China has proclaimed freedom and equality for all, and the United States has unhappily limited itself "to freedom for some peoples, but not for others, to the four lesser freedoms, not freedom itself."[16]

While Pearl Buck continued to enlighten Americans about Asian attitudes and feelings and about the real meaning of the battle against the Axis, she also, with particular emphasis during the war years, attempted to make the people see the folly of their treatment of blacks. In a famous and widely circulated letter to the *New York Times*, she objected to a *Times* editorial that discussed a crime wave in Harlem and recommended only general measures of correction. Following the problem to its roots, Buck pinpointed the whole matter as a question of racial prejudice. She noted that blacks are prevented from obtaining many jobs, from entering certain labor unions, from receiving equal pay for an equal amount of work, and from living in better neighborhoods. Even in defense industries the black is often unable to receive the same amount of pay or the same kind of jobs that white workers do.[17] The segregation policies in the armed services are also cited as unjust and unfair. Buck remarked that the blacks in the United States have often been told that, if they are patient and humble, they will eventually be accepted on an equal basis. Now, however, they are coming to understand the futility and hopelessness of such a position—to lose patience with the status quo. Many white people in the United States, Buck maintained, want to retain a master-servant relationship with the black. But this relationship is not democracy, and it should be eliminated from the nation's thinking.

In an open letter sent to all Negro magazines and newspapers in America and in Canada and later anthologized, Pearl Buck attempted to assuage the anger and frustrations of black Americans. She urged American blacks to support the war effort wholeheartedly even though they have not received the benefits of democracy. She attacked the Japanese propaganda theme of colored people united against whites. She neither excused nor condoned past and present injustices, but she insisted that a majority of white Americans was coming to understand the viciousness of prejudice and to realize that prejudice must be discarded. She argued that the beliefs of this group would supersede those of fascistic-minded Americans who are the enemies of democracy. Her prediction has happily proved to be valid.

Pearl Buck's wartime speaking and writing considered other questions of freedom and equality. She protested against mistreatment of Japanese-Americans and urged that they be treated with fairness and consideration. She asked Japanese-Americans to understand and to forgive irrational and unthinking attitudes on the part of individual citizens and the American government.[18] She discussed the question of India frequently. She supported freedom and independence for India; and, while recording the problem of lack of unity in India, she remarked that the British are not solving this dilemma.[19] At one time Britain could have won India's complete loyalty and support, but that time is past; India must have the right to govern itself, to establish its ruling program while ruling itself, learning by trial and error. India has waited for its independence for one hundred and fifty years, and promises for the future mean very little at the moment. Freedom is what India wants and needs now.[20] Again, the passing of time has demonstrated Buck's prescience.

Another publicized treatise by Pearl Buck during the war years was directed to America's churches. Noting the theoretical position of churches to stress man's freedom and brotherhood, Buck finds that many people put such factors as the maintenance of imperialism, the continuance of Jim Crowism, and the insistence on Oriental exclusion from America ahead of basic human equality. She insists that it is the duty of the churches to furnish the leadership that will make this war a true success against a Nazi way of life. The churches should take a forceful stand against racial prejudice and campaign to put into practice the doctrine of human brotherhood. Such a movement would not only help our war effort throughout the world but could be the foundation of a just and lasting peace at the end of the war; for "any treaty which is not based upon human equality and implemented on human equality will bring the world no peace."[21] Buck wonders if religion and the churches are really dead. If they are not, now is the important and proper psychological time to proclaim the duty of equality and brotherhood.

Another emphatic trend of Buck's thought in the World War II years was her insistence that Americans should not yield their democratic privileges during wartime.[22] An influential school of thought during the war years persisted in the belief that the government should not be criticized while engaged in its struggle against fascism: people should be reluctant to be frank and to complain because to do so would put our country in danger. Pearl Buck, who maintains that this viewpoint is incorrect, asserts that freedom of speech must not be surrendered since it is a fundamental democratic guarantee and safeguard against totalitarianism. "The beginning of fascism has always been the attempt to suppress intelligent inquiry and the moment this suppression is successful, intellectuals are put into prison and killed and the books are burned."[23] It would be ironic indeed, if while we were fighting against fascism abroad, we should give refuge to its principles at home.

In the light of subsequent events, both abroad and at home, Pearl Buck's views were filled with foresight and a basic awareness of trends and features that have come to pass. One must lament the fact that her constant warnings and insights too often went unheeded. Yet the fact that her predictions have come to pass and that not enough readers and listeners heeded her ideas in no way invalidates her efforts. On the contrary, her nonfiction writings demonstrate a mature, intelligent, and thoughtful mind—and one far ahead of its time. Today many of Buck's remarks on the injustice of imperialism and on the need for racial equality and justice seem almost platitudinous in their logic and sense. Such ideas possess an immediacy and a timeliness which beggars description. Pearl Buck has always attempted to shake America out of an isolated, limited viewpoint and to force it to recognize its commitment to the world and to the principle of freedom everywhere.

IV   Dragon Seed

Pearl Buck's wartime activities were not divorced from her creative efforts in fiction. This fact can be demonstrated by a reading of *Dragon Seed*, one of her best-known and most popular works. In a monograph issued for presentation by the East and West Association, Buck explains the genesis of this novel.[24] Well acquainted with the farming families who lived near Nanking, she learned of their reaction to the horrors of the Japanese invasion. For the first time in history these Chinese farmers witnessed destructive bombing from airplanes, the wanton killing of innocent civilians, and bestial attacks on very young and very old women. Accustomed as they were to frequent bandit skirmishes and to warlord raids, the farmers in the Nanking area had never beheld any cruelty so intense and so indiscriminate. The conduct of the Japanese generated a resistance movement among the populace, a movement which came to harass and vex the enemy unceasingly. From information about the Japanese conquest and its concomitant inhumanity, Buck constructed the basic framework for the story of *Dragon Seed*.

The narrative centers around the farmer Ling Tan and his family, who live in a village three miles from Nanking. Ling Tan has three sons and two daughters, the elder girl being married to a merchant in the city. Ling's sons help him in the fields, and the family leads the usual rural life, living close to the soil and toiling diligently. Ling Tan has the same affection for his land that Wang Lung possessed, and he faces the same agricultural problems and concerns. At this period the Japanese invasion is remote and practically nonexistent. But as time passes the Ling family and their neighbors are brought to a much greater awareness of the war. Scores of refugees stream past Nanking and the Ling village on their way to the inner provinces of China, and rumors of Japanese atrocities spread throughout the countryside. Bombers begin to visit Nanking with increasing regularity, and the people, who on the first occasion beheld the airplanes with curiosity and admiration, come suddenly to fear the death and destruction rained from the skies. When the Japanese troops themselves reach Nanking and the surrounding area, their barbarian behavior shocks the conquered people. One of Ling Tan's own sons is violated by several lust-crazed soldiers. The conduct of the Japanese, plus the imposition of heavy taxation and other restrictive regulations, nourishes the Chinese underground movement. Although the main strength of the Chinese resistance fighters is centered in the nearby hills, each village participates in every way possible, taking every opportunity to kill the Japanese. Ling Tan's three sons join the underground, and Ling Tan himself becomes the village leader in these activities.

What is to this point a realistic, convincing, and perceptive narrative suddenly veers into a wild adventure yarn. Lao San, Ling Tan's third son, is now a ruthless guerrilla leader in the hills. Even his men realize that he needs a woman to soften some of his energy and passion. Lao San, however, is an extremely handsome, complacent individual who scorns ordinary women. What he is looking for, as his family remarks with amusement, is a goddess. Such a woman soon appears. Her name is Mayli, and she is attractive, independent, well educated, and willful. At one point she compares herself to Madame Chiang Kai-shek, who, doubtless, furnished the inspiration for the author's original conception of Mayli.[25] The daughter of a Chinese official in a foreign capital, Mayli decides to return to her native land in order to help her people against the Japanese. At first she acquires a teaching position at a girls' school in the inner regions of China; but, demanding a more militant and guerrilla-minded training for her students, she soon quarrels with the principal and is dismissed. While at this school, however, she has met Pansiao, Lao San's younger sister, who tells her of her brother's qualities and of his search for a wife. Mayli's romantic interests are aroused. Through a series of improbable authorial manipulations, Mayli manages to come to Ling Tan's house, and there she meets Lao San. Mayli and Lao San are attracted to each other, and Lao San makes arrangements to join her in unoccupied territory inland.

The Mayli episode is the chief factor in the failure of *Dragon Seed* to achieve artistic success. The Mayli incident is a disastrous attempt to insert romantic materials into a context of realism. The novel concludes by stressing that guerrilla warfare will continue, and radio news suggests a promise of Allied help against the Japanese. The impact of the theme is weakened by a Hollywood touch designed to bring romantic interest into the latter part of the novel.

Pearl Buck's handling of the Mayli material illustrates a pitfall of the natural storyteller's technique—a pitfall to which Buck succumbs more and more in her post-Nobel Prize work and which comes to blemish most of the later novels at some point or other. The traditional storyteller—the balladeer, the narrator around the camp-fire, the Arabian Nights spellbinder, even the amateur at the children's bedside—can justify almost any touch. In order to prevent lagging attention, the storyteller justifies the inclusion of the most marvelous, fantastic, and improbable happenings. The more serious and more artistic novelist, however, must answer for such improbabilities, and here we have the principal weakness displayed in *Dragon Seed*. Make-believe romance has intruded on basically realistic material and has reduced the impact of authenticity of event and logic of character portrayal.

Another defect displayed in *Dragon Seed* is a conscious attempt to use the novel as a vehicle for patriotic propaganda. This aspect is most obvious in the radio news scenes which bring the Chinese a knowledge that their fight is part of a worldwide struggle against evil. The people and the resistance fighters, cheered by this information, are now more inclined to resist the enemy; and the novel comes to a conclusion with the hope of British and American support. Although

Dragon Seed was published on January 22, 1942, it was completed before the Allied powers entered the war against Japan; it was predicated on the need and desirability of more active support for China, and it definitely had been intended to arouse sympathy for the Chinese cause.

While the intrusion of farfetched romance and evident propaganda mar the novel, *Dragon Seed* contains much to make it worthwhile. Its most attractive feature is its style. Pearl Buck had not used the early semi-biblical, semi-traditional style since *A House Divided*. This prose, particularly effective in *The Good Earth*, is handled with considerable success in *Dragon Seed*. Simple, often poetic, pliable, fitting the material with a picturesqueness, the prose of *Dragon Seed* satisfies both the eye and ear. Many of the passages could, with a few word changes, seem to be the work of Hemingway. For example, the following passage describing some of the reactions after the first Japanese bombing raid on Nanking is not far from the tone and manner of *A Farewell to Arms*:

The next day the flying ships came back again and the day after that, and again on the next day and the next, and every day they came back and the city was scourged by death and by fire. But Ling Tan did not go there again, nor did any of his house. They stayed where they were and tended their crops and put by their food for the winter as they did in every other year. The only change they would allow the enemy was that when the ships came over their heads now they left the field and hid themselves in the bamboos. For one day a flying ship had dipped low like a swallow over a pool, and had cut the head clean from a farmer who stood staring at it.[26]

In the sustained excellence of its style *Dragon Seed* comes close to *The Good Earth*; its prose does not, however, possess as much poetry and color as Buck's most famous novel.

Other similarities between *Dragon Seed* and *The Good Earth* are apparent. The same deep feeling for the value of the land is present in both books, and the same quiet tone and the chronological approach concentrating on the lives of two generations characterize the two novels. *The Good Earth*, however, rises to several climaxes; *Dragon Seed* tends to move in an even, steady manner without crucial elevations of interest. Both stories contain a realism which, at times, verges on Zola-like Naturalism. The violation of Ling Tan's son has considerable shock value, and the raping and mutilation of the merchant Wu Lien's ancient and obese mother exploits sensational matter for a telling effect. The novel renders Japanese behavior vividly and disturbingly. If, in fact, *Dragon Seed* had kept to a more probable story line, divorced romance from realism, and retained the authorial objectivity demonstrated in *The Good Earth*, it could have rivaled Buck's Pulitzer Prize novel in several ways.

V The Promise

The Promise (1943), a sequel to *Dragon Seed*, deals primarily with the Chinese campaign in Burma. While Ling Tan and his family continue their lives under the enemy occupation, he awaits the promise of help from England and the United States to be fulfilled for his country. Meanwhile, Lao San, his third son, goes to the free section of China and participates in several battles culminating in the victory of Long Sands. Lao San is renamed Sheng by his military superior and is raised in rank. Allied strategy calls for the Chinese to send soldiers to Burma in order to aid the British forces, who are under heavy attack by the Japanese. Sheng is chosen to lead a group of men in this campaign. Going along on the trip to Burma is Mayli, the All-Universe Wonder Woman whose appearance shattered the latter part of *Dragon Seed*. She heads a contingent of nurses. The Chinese troops trek over the Burma Road; but, when they reach the border of Burma, they are held there for several weeks, although it is obvious to everyone that the harassed British need immediate support.

By the time the Chinese are allowed to enter the action, the crucial port of Rangoon has fallen, and the British are disorganized and in retreat. The belated call to the Chinese and lack of coordination between the Allied units result in constant and costly withdrawals. Finally, the Chinese are called upon to support the British retreat over the Irrawaddy River. After the British and Chinese troops have crossed the river to safety, plans call for the bridge to be destroyed so that the besieging Japanese cannot immediately follow. The Chinese fight valiantly and enable the British to get over the bridge; however, the British destroy the bridge prematurely, and the bulk of the Chinese troops, caught with no means of escape, are then slaughtered. Sheng and a few others survive and set out for the trip back to China, but the Chinese are disillusioned by the conduct of the British and by the refusal of the white men to treat them as genuine equals and allies.

The Promise is history fictionalized. The long wait by the Chinese soldiers on the Burma border, their entry into the battle when it was too late to turn the side, the destruction of the bridge and the ensuing entrapment of the Chinese—these and several other events are true occurrences. The book thus takes on historical importance because it is a thoughtful, challenging explanation of the disaster that overtook the Chinese in Burma. At the time of the Burma debacle many observers and correspondents believed that the delayed entry of the Chinese troops occurred because of color prejudice: the British wished to prevent the Burmese and the Indians serving in Burma from viewing native forces led by native officers. It was also charged that the Chinese were used as cover to save the fleeing British units. This viewpoint is still held in some quarters.

The "official" view of the disaster—remembering, however, one character's comment in *The Promise*, "You white men . . . are determined to save each other's faces"[27]—ascribes the rout to tactical errors and poor military planning. It appears, nevertheless, that both Pearl Buck's charges and the official explanations enter into the complete picture of what happened. What cannot be denied is the disillusionment of the Chinese with the treatment received from the British. Admittedly, some racial prejudice was in evidence and admittedly too the British were not committed with full will to the campaign, for there was no realization that Burma was the lifeline to China. With the fall of Burma, the Burma Road was cut; supplies to China from then on could be sent only by air, and China's plight worsened. In one of her essays Pearl Buck speaks of firsthand witnesses who indicated that the British were not particularly concerned about digging in and retaining control of Burma at all costs.[28]

The Promise is, in almost every way, out-and-out propaganda, a patriotic and stirring appeal for the Chinese cause. The prejudice of the white men, their feelings of superiority over Asians, their refusal to treat the Chinese with equality, the harm that these attitudes were causing in the war against Japan—these matters are reiterated throughout the novel. The book also proclaims the worthiness of the Chinese for aid, although, up to this time, they had received little in the way of planes and other necessary military equipment. The Flying Tigers are, nevertheless, given favorable mention.

Since *The Promise* is so dominated by propaganda, it possesses little artistic value. The incredible love affair between Sheng and Mayli outrages the reader. Mayli has come originally to China to help the Chinese cause, but in the latter part of *Dragon Seed* and in the early part of this novel she is a woman with only romance on her mind. She seems to be able to enplane anywhere almost at will (in some ways she could come out of the plays of G. B. Shaw), and the device of having her go along on the Burma trek as an unofficial observer for Madame Chiang Kai-shek is so obviously rigged and false that it tends to discredit belief in the novel's verisimilitude. The survival of Sheng and Mayli and their chance meeting near the end are also embarrassingly manipulated. Again the romantic interest has vitiated the essential realism of the setting. The Mayli-Sheng affair makes Edmund Wilson's delicious comment about another book neatly applicable here: "This novel," Wilson remarked, "was constructed with an eye to the demands of Hollywood, that intractable magnetic mountain which has been twisting our fiction askew and on which so many writers have been flattened."[29]

The style of *The Promise* is in the vein of *Dragon Seed*, but it is obviously much more hastily written, flat, and less poetic. On occasion, some of the prose is appealing. This passage, for example, captures the flavor of Pearl Buck's finest work:

Wounded men and whole, all were alike, and what the enemy in the sky did not do, the enemy pressing furiously from the earth finished. In so little time that the sun had scarcely crept above the clouds, the battle was over, and the enemy vehicles and the marching men and the airplanes were sweeping furiously northward, a typhoon of men and metal. And what lay behind lay unburied by the road that ran through the jungle.[30]

The principal interest in *The Promise* is not a stylistic but historical one. This book is a fictionalized, partly true document of a significant campaign in World War II, and whether the novel's main thesis is accepted in full or in part, the book makes a convincing case for its point of view.

CHAPTER 7

Perspectives of East and West

I *Enter John Sedges*

NEITHER of Pearl Buck's seriously intended American novels had been received with particular favor by critics.[1] It became a platitude to claim that she could not write successful novels about American subject matter. As she familiarized herself with people and places in the United States, she desired to make use of American materials; but she felt that she had been labeled as a writer about China and that, accordingly, her American work would not receive a fair hearing. She decided upon a pseudonym: "I chose the name of John Sedges, a simple one, and masculine because men have fewer handicaps in our society than women have in writing as well as in other professions."[2] The name John was selected on the basis of its commonness while the surname Sedges was chosen because it was fresh and unused.[3] There was also a commercial consideration since she was writing books faster than her publishers thought it was financially wise to issue them.

Five novels were published under the pseudonym of John Sedges: *The Townsman* (1945), *The Angry Wife* (1947), *The Long Love* (1949), *Bright Procession* (1952), and *Voices in the House* (1953). In 1958 in the preface of a collected edition of three of these novels, Buck declared that she was giving up her nom de plume, that she felt free at last to write on either American or Chinese themes, that "People are people whether in Asia or America, as everybody knows or ought to know, and for me the scene is merely the background for human antics."[4]

Only one of the John Sedges books, *The Townsman*, is of especial importance. Unless a person had inside information, he would never guess that Pearl Buck authored *The Townsman* since the settings and characters are totally different from those found in her previous books on American subjects.[5] The story takes place primarily in and

around Median, Kansas, during the pioneering years of the nineteenth and early twentieth centuries.

The finest feature of the book is its success in presenting the
authentic flavor of the early settlements in the West. The first sight of
an embryo Kansas hamlet bogged in heavy, sucking mud is
unforgettable. The construction of sod houses, the prairie fire, the
blizzards, the revival meeting, the beginning of boardwalks, the first
planting of town trees, the effect of the severe hardships of frontier
life on a sensitive woman such as Mary Goodliffe—these and similar
matters are captured with convincing realism.

The novel is scrupulously researched. Pearl Buck traveled to
Kansas in order to obtain background and to study the history and
people of the region. Richard Walsh, her second husband, was born
in Kansas, and he added his knowledge of the locale to hers. The
authenticity of the material has been acknowledged by Kansans.[6]

In addition to the realism of background details and of some of the
basic incidents, the dialogue in *The Townsman* evinces much credibility. Considerable attention is given to dialectal forms, to picturesque expressions, and to quaint oddities of word choice and sentence
construction. The style of the book does not distinguish itself except
where the dialectal elements and the picturesque speech give the novel
a pleasantly natural coloring. The nondialogue writing does not
consist of the semi-biblical style found in the early novels about
China; it is rather a commonplace and undistinguished prose most
similar to the style used in *Other Gods*.

While much of *The Townsman* attracts because of its realistic
flavor, the book also possesses definite appeal because of its central
character—Jonathan Goodliffe. Jonathan is a thoughtful, prudent,
upright individual "too ready to think of work instead of play."[7]
Before he left England, he had studied to be a school teacher; and he
takes up this calling as soon as he can in frontier Kansas. Not only
must he be a teacher to his students, he must be a parent in absentia.
He must perform such extracurricular duties as forcing a young pupil
to wash—he achieves this feat by reciting the first words of Virgil's
Aeneid, pretending to cast a spell over the lad and, thus, frightens him
into capitulation—and preventing some of his older scholars from
drinking in the local tavern-hotel.

At the same time, Jonathan serves as the town planner. He wants
Median to develop into a sedate county seat, not a wild, lawless cattle
town. He knows the appeal of a good school building on migrating
families: "It's the schoolhouse gets 'em. A woman with kids sees a

school, and then heaven and hell and all her menfolk can't drawr her past."[8] He does not concern himself with formal religions, but he insists that the community should have a church and he works toward this end. Not only does he do everything he can to uphold standards in the development of the town, but he strictly governs his own personal life and stresses respectability. Jilted by the only woman who ever caught his romantic interest, Jonathan marries Katie Merridy without loving her. Although their union is far from completely satisfying, Jonathan does his best to stand by his hard-working but insensitive wife. He reflects that another man in the same position would probably leave his wife, but he realizes that he cares "too much for what I've built up here in Median."[9] In his old age Jonathan has the satisfaction of having his love of Median replace his lifelong affection for the girl who rejected him. The town, "the creation of his being," becomes what he planned it "should be, the seat of a prosperous farming county."[10]

That Median, Kansas, shows signs of eventually turning into a Gopher Prairie should not detract from Jonathan's achievement. Only through efforts of civic-minded individuals could a stable community develop. That such as Jonathan Goodliffe always had their influence in the early West cannot be denied, but their lives are usually overlooked in literary accounts which focus on the more glamorous aspects of sheriffs, marshals, rustlers, and Indians. In his study of *The American Historical Novel*, Ernest Leisy notes that *The Townsman* stands as one of the turning points in an attempt by the American historical novelist to de-emphasize the more sensational aspects of frontier existence and to concentrate on the solid and decent citizens who were instrumental in molding their particular communities.[11] Pearl Buck was weary of cowboy stories of the early West, and she decided to portray the more constructive side of pioneering.

Jonathan Goodliffe is well depicted. His motives and feelings make sense; his life, his ideas, and his influence on the life of Median possess the genuine feel of truth. Unfortunately, he is too drab and colorless an individual to make a Dickensian impact on the reader's consciousness. Like many "good" people in fiction, he eventually becomes something of a bore. From time to time he demonstrates a flair for capturing the fancy, but these outbursts are sporadic and not sustained long enough to render him memorable.

The Townsman has value as a chronology of an American pioneering family and of the growth of a prairie town; however, it is weakened by several story improbabilities, by several type characters, and by some overly obvious propaganda. Jonathan's brother Jamie, a restless, ne'er-do-well lad, marries an aristocratic Southern belle and becomes an important figure in a large oil company. Jamie thus becomes the brother-in-law of lawyer Evan Bayne, the man who eloped with Jonathan's beloved Judy Spender. Jamie's ascent in the world and his connection with the Baynes are much too coincidental and incredible for acceptance. Evan, the suave, handsome aristocrat, and Judy, the selfish, empty-headed beauty, are just two of several stereotyped characters who have recurred too often in too many novels to arouse any particular interest.

The Parrys, an assiduous and neighborly Negro family who migrated to Kansas after the Civil War, are shown to be the victims of racial prejudice even though they now live in a "free" state. Stephen Parry's brilliant stepson Beaumont, with Jonathan's help and some rather farfetched turns of plotting, becomes a gifted surgeon in France. There, and we are not allowed to forget this point, he is not discriminated against because of his color. The sermon about racial prejudice in America jars the story line out of logical development and pushes some of the characters to a secondary role since they exist not in or for themselves but simply to help draw a moral. Didactic concerns mar certain parts of the book.

The novel's presentation often lacks vitality, particularly in several of the middle sections; and the tone is underplayed throughout. It is almost as if this paean to pioneering America and to its upright citizen is deliberately muted so that a false note of emotionalism will not intrude. Nevertheless, sentimentalism is present; and, although it is held in check for the most part, it is never too far away. It blows over the story from time to time. This factor, together with sporadic moralizing, gives the work a softness if could better do without. How these features would have blurred *The Good Earth* if they had been allowed to enter that excellent book!

When Buck writes in a true-to-life manner, her portraits are effective. In episodes such as the muddy arrival of the Goodliffes in Median, the picture of family living in a primitive sod house, and the Willa Cather situation of the civilized mother struggling against an antagonistic environment, Buck captures much of the biting realistic feeling for pioneer life that distinguishes, say, Edgar Watson Howe's *The Story of a Country Town*, a novel which shares the same locale. Unlike Howe, Pearl Buck dilutes the strength of her canvas with an assuasive romanticism which makes the scene unreal. The intrusion of dashing Evan Bayne, the tepid Judy Spender, Beaumont's rags-to-riches ascent, and similar elements forfeit probability; and this note of the romantic that clashes with the realism diminishes one's final impression of the novel, and forces it to a second-rate status.

This mixture of the real and the romantic doubtless accounts for *The Townsman*'s popularity with the reading public. Its interest for literary history and for students of Pearl Buck's work rests on its ability in many passages to portray with authority the birth of a pioneer community and the influence on this town of one dedicated, public-spirited citizen. A place for such a subject in American fiction definitely exists, and Buck has in part rendered this topic with persuasiveness. Aside from this factor, *The Townsman* is of interest in studying Pearl Buck's career because several of its characteristics— both strengths and weaknesses—are typical of the later John Sedges novels, no matter how much they vary in subject and in setting.

All of the John Sedges books are competently written, but only several sections of *The Townsman* and the vivid portrait of a minor character, Lew Harrow, in *The Long Love* exceed mere journeyman competence. Pearl Buck proves that she can write entertainingly and informatively on a wide variety of American subjects, but the John Sedges novels display relatively little depth or effectively realized characterization. The overemphasis on message and the general feeling of elation that everything will turn out all right give them a Victorian quality that often rests on sentimentalism and is unworthy of the talent behind their conception.

The John Sedges novels are also characterized by the good man as hero: the solid citizen; the loyal husband; the decent, upright individual—a type that obviously appeals to Buck. In addition to Jonathan Goodliffe, there is Tom and Pierce Delaney (in *The Angry Wife*), Edward Haslatt (in *The Long Love*), William Asher (in *Voices in the House*), and Stephen Worth (in *Bright Procession*), two of the names immediately suggesting their qualities. Jonathan Goodliffe is the most convincing of the group; for in his time, place, intentions, and activities, he seems quite logically drawn. Haslatt and Asher, while stuffy, old-fashioned, and somewhat remote, are credible in the context of their particular stories. The Delaneys and Worth, however, are cardboard figures; they are drawn in an obviously manipulated, superficial, and dimensionless manner.

II Pavilion of Women

While Pearl Buck was writing the John Sedges novels, she was also producing others under her own name. Among her most popular efforts during this period was *Pavilion of Women*. Madame Wu, the matron of an aristocratic and influential Chinese family, is the central figure in this novel. Indirectly, two generations of the family are studied but always with Madame Wu in the forefront. Although her husband is paterfamilias, Madame Wu manages the household and oversees the vast agricultural interests belonging to the Wu clan. A wise and intelligent woman, Madame Wu has never really loved her husband, but she has been a model wife, performing all her obligations faithfully and binding the family to herself with strong ties. When she reaches her fortieth birthday, she astounds both her husband and the family by announcing that she does not wish to bear more children. (In a well-to-do traditional Chinese family the day on which a woman reached forty was often a day of decision and the beginning of a new way of life. When, for example, Madame Wu's mother-in-law reached forty, she had turned the management of the family affairs over to her only son's wife.) Madame Wu is fearful of having a child after forty and does not wish to have further sexual relations with her husband. Knowing that her husband's sexual interests are undiminished, Madame Wu determines to provide a concubine for him. She carefully chooses a kind, tractable, uneducated country girl and instructs her in her responsibilities. At first Madame Wu's husband rejects the suggestion that he take another woman; but, when he realizes that his wife is adamant in her resolve, he assents.

Now that Madame Wu is relieved of physical concerns, which were distasteful to her sensitive and fastidious nature, she is free to cultivate her mind. She intends to emancipate herself from the problems of others and to develop her individuality and personal interests to the fullest.

Soon, in the course of helping one of her sons, she engages a tutor. This man, who calls himself Brother André, is a priest defrocked because of heretical beliefs. Brother André lives in the town and directs a foundling home. As her son Fengmo comes under André's tutelage, the influence of the priest's high-minded thinking is felt both by his pupil and by Madame Wu. She too decides to study under André. André realizes that she is a deeply unhappy woman who has found little meaning to life. He opens her mind and heart to new intellectual and spiritual knowledge. She questions him closely about his religion and learns that his life is based completely on humanitarianism. He helps his fellowman in every possible way and attempts to lead a gentle, charitable existence.

Madame Wu's respect for Brother André and his way of life increases; but, while she pursues her studies, the household begins to disintegrate. Quarrels between her sons and their wives break out, and Mr. Wu becomes dissatisfied with Ch'iuming, his concubine, and turns his attention to a flower house girl. With Brother André's guidance, Madame Wu probes her unhappiness and the disorganization and dissatisfaction in the family. In cutting herself off from her husband and partly from her family she insists that she had wanted to be free of unnecessary responsibilities, to manage her affairs without demands from anyone else. André maintains that she has treated her husband improperly, that she has regarded the concubine solely as a piece of property to be bought or sold at will, and that she has placed herself on a superior level to all other women. André urges her to forget herself, to de-emphasize and subordinate selfishness. Madame Wu then acknowledges that she has never really loved anyone. No one has ever pleased her, and she has always been too quick to find faults and weaknesses in other people. In considering the question of love she recalls André's teaching and the words, "Love thy neighbor as thyself"; she had protested that the word *love* was really "too strong," and he had responded: "The word is too strong . . . you are right. . . . Love is not the word. No one can love his neighbor. Say, rather, 'know thy neighbor as thyself.' That is, comprehend his hardships and understand his position, deal with his faults as gently as with your own. Do not judge him where you do not judge yourself . . . this is the meaning of the word *love*."[12]

After Brother André's death—while trying to assist a shop owner, he is accidentally killed by robbers—Madame Wu believes that she had fallen in love with him. From then on he becomes her guiding spirit. She thinks of his ideas constantly, attempts to put them into practice, and does all she can to arrange satisfactory solutions to the various problems besetting the household. She manages to have the flower house girl whom Mr. Wu now loves come and live with the family as the Third Lady. She settles the differences between her sons and their wives in as amicable a manner as possible, and takes over the care of the homeless children whom André had befriended. As she grows in her consideration for others, her selfishness recedes, and she becomes more content and satisfied. Now she lets love dominate her existence, and she no longer allows herself to retain a dislike for ordinary human beings.

In her autobiography Buck makes special mention of the many letters she received from women in all parts of the world who acknowledged the book's appeal, and the book does have much to recommend it.[13] First of all, the style is poetic, lush, and colorful. Deliberately romantic in tone, it is most reminiscent of the first part of *East Wind: West Wind.* While the style is often exuberant and exotic, it is in perfect keeping with its subject matter. The setting of an old, rich, and comfortable Chinese family receives an added luster and charm as the style blends perfectly with the scene. Second, Pearl Buck evinces as much knowledge of the customs and activities of a wealthy Chinese family as she does of the peasant groups. The background and details are thorough and convincing; time and place sweep into the mind with genuine verisimilitude. Third, *Pavilion of Women* exists as one of the most vivid demonstrations of Buck's uncanny ability to invent fresh episodes and to entangle her characters in imaginative situations which exemplify never-flagging interest, variety, and considerable narrative pull.

Because of the significance of the theme—the question of personal meaning and immortality—and its excellent style, *Pavilion of Women* should be an important and memorable novel. Such is not the case. Its failure stems from an overly evident manipulation of the narrative to support Buck's didactic purpose: to prove the value of selfless love and devotion to others. When Madame Wu adopts André's philosophy, her kindness and understanding too suddenly diffuse through the book. Seemingly insoluble problems are either resolved easily or simply pacified. Every knot can be untied or loosened if one acts with selfless intent and altruistic consideration, the author too obviously implies. And, while the reader would like this to be true, he knows from experience that this is simply not true— or at least not in as uncomplicated a way as Buck would have it. An oversimplification and an unfortunate sentimentalism have set in. A sentimentalism, which she would have scorned to use in books such as *The Good Earth* and *The Mother*, unfortunately, came to the forefront more and more often in Pearl Buck's post-1939 fiction.

Another noticeable weakness of this novel is that neither of its two principal characters—Madame Wu and Brother André—is really credible. Madame Wu's reformation is not convincing. The reader does not see the change; he is simply told about it, although, of course, he sees the result of the change. Perhaps the type of narration is primarily at fault. The reader is *told* too much; he does not really see or feel enough. A more internal analysis of Madame Wu's mind and thought processes—much deeper and more gradual than is given—would render her character development more acceptable and believable. Madame Wu becomes, too suddenly and too unrealistically, Lady Bountiful; and her ability to rectify most of the problems she and her family face is nothing short of fantastic.

One would like to believe in Brother André. Certainly he is a saint and a fictional exemplar of Buck's own humanitarianism. Preaching—and more important than that—living a life of kindness, selflessness, and good deeds, André exists as an ideal model of what Buck hopes every man could emulate. But the old artistic problem of trying to give flesh and bones to such an ideal creation recurs in her portrayal of André. It is always much easier for a writer to give an evil character life than a good character; for a classic example, Satan outshines Adam in Milton's *Paradise Lost*. Brother André appears as a fanciful dream, a wish-fulfillment, a strange, exotic creature who belongs more appropriately in the fantastic world of James Hilton's Shangri-La than in real life. This is a pity, for it took considerable imagination to conceive of André, and he possesses an inherent strength to hold the reader's attention. Perhaps if more thought had been given to his development and more analysis to his character, he might have become a memorable realization.

One final point of interest remains. Madame Wu, although a skeptic in regard to religious matters, becomes convinced of André's immortality: that André continues to exist, that he will continue to dwell within her. Love has brought her to a spiritual transcendence. Formal religious dogmas or other aspects of spiritual interest had never affected her, but now her love for André has raised her to mystical heights. She now believes that after her death her own soul will live on; love has persuaded her.

The similarity between this fictional situation and Pearl Buck's personal views as expressed in *A Bridge for Passing* is striking. This nonfictional work, which deals principally with her reaction to the death of her husband Richard Walsh, expresses a faith in the immortality of the soul.[14] This question she has treated only rarely in her written work, but it is evident that her thought is stimulated by the belief that the spirit continues to live with energy after death. Love has carried her thought to this conclusion.

III Kinfolk

With the important exception of a relatively brief section of *A House Divided* and such novels as *Other Gods* and *China Gold*, Pearl Buck generally kept her work on American and Chinese subject matter separated. Relatively late in her writing career, however, she produced several novels of descriptive value and thematic interest in which the worlds of the West and the East met within the pages of one book. The possibilities for illuminating comparison and contrast between two countries, which she had, up to this point, largely subordinated to portraits of one area, are best exemplified in *Kinfolk*. This book presents the story of the Liang family. Dr. Liang was reared in China, but he is now a well-known teacher of Chinese philosophy at a New York City college. His oldest son James graduates from an American medical school and angers his father by informing him that he wants to practice his profession in China. James hopes to help the people of China. He leaves for the Far East and takes a position in a Peking hospital. Later, when Dr. Liang's youngest daughter Louise gets involved with an American boy, the father sends her and his two other children to China. James and his equally idealistic sister Mary decide to live in Anming, the ancestral village of the Liang family.

Anming is a place of dirt and mud and almost unbelievable primitiveness, but both young people desire a link with their heritage and wish to use a grass-roots approach to helping the Chinese villagers. With the aid of their granduncle Tao, James opens and conducts a small clinic while Mary attempts to teach reading and writing. These two Liang children expect to participate in the rebirth of their ancestral homeland.

Kinfolk excels in underscoring the division between the Chinese peasant and the intellectual Chinese living in America. Dr. Liang believes that he is a transmitter of Confucian enlightenment to American students. Only scholars and intellectuals are significant as far as he is concerned. He is a thorough-going snob who sneers at the ordinary Chinese, refuses to admit that the peasants form the bulk of China's population, and denies that such customs as footbinding of women were carried on in the twentieth century. Liang is unquestionably modeled on such Chinese intellectuals as Kiang Kang-Hu and others who attacked the accuracy of *The Good Earth*. When Dr. Liang's son Peter goes to China and finds out the true condition of that country, he is disillusioned with his father's theories and joins some student revolutionaries. Peter is eventually killed by government police. Reflecting on Peter's death, Dr. Liang realizes that he had deliberately allowed his children "to grow up with a sentimental notion of what China was like. He had even helped to make the notion. . . . But he had wanted the children to understand the glory of

China, the honor, the dignity of an ancient race and country. He himself purposely dwelled upon these things."[15]

What applies to Dr. Liang in America, also applies, the novel demonstrates, to the upper classes in China. For centuries the scholars, as well as the landlords and magistrates, have held themselves above the common people and have oppressed them. This alliance of tyranny and snobbery has led to a reaction against such heartless inhumanity, and this reaction has resulted in Communism.

Dr. Liang's daughter Louise is completely dissimilar to James and Mary. She dislikes China and is absolutely American in her manner and preference. She represents the feelings of the typical young Chinese-American. While many of their elders think of returning to China, most of the youthful Chinese-Americans in New York City are quite happy with their adopted country and have no wish to leave the United States. In scenes in New York's Chinatown and in circles of the wealthier Chinese living in Manhattan, there is either a divided or an ambivalent reaction toward China.

Several similarities and contrasts between China and America are emphasized in the novel. Mary Liang, for instance, living in a small Chinese village and married to a native Chinese, is a dominant, forceful teacher and leader, who behaves like an American and inspires a sense of independence in some native Chinese women. Louise, on the other hand, married to an American and living in New York, becomes an old-fashioned Chinese wife, thoroughly subordinate and docile toward her husband, justifying her mother's observation that the world at the present time is a greatly disordered place. That the division into poor and wealthy applies both to the United States and to China is another thesis that is given decided emphasis. Wherever a division exists, however, bridges are found. Dr. Liang's wife, for example, serves as a bridge between Anming's and Uncle Tao's eighteenth-century primitiveness and James and Mary's modernity. Mrs. Liang possesses a humanity and a concern that can comprehend both viewpoints. She is a balance in "a world where new and old had to live together on their differing levels."[16]

While Dr. Liang has cut himself off from the bulk of China's population, his son James settles down to the life of a village doctor. James now knows that "there was no magic homeland . . . [only] poverty and oppression, and indifference to both";[17] nevertheless, he and Mary are practical and energetic enough to help improve some of the backward conditions they encounter. James marries a peasant girl. Whenever people were afraid of medical treatment, he could bridge the gap through his wife Yumei, who was one of the people's own. Only through an alliance of the intellectuals and peasants can China improve in education, economics, and medicine, the novel implies. But it is Buck's belief that the intellectual must have the peasant as the root of his own existence. It is Dr. Liang's earthy wife who supplies the basis that gives his life meaning. James Liang reaches contentment, truth, and his raison d'être through the peasant Yumei.

Although its plot is too plainly contrived, *Kinfolk* is critically interesting because it is an amalgam of the strong and weak points in Buck's later work. The main themes are well conceived and credible. The picture of life in Anming is exceptionally vivid, instructive, and meaningful; the characteristics of the hamlet stand forth with stark boldness. The scenes in America are less persuasive, although the Chinatown impressions furnish novelty. Unfortunately, too many popular touches are mixed into the ingredients. The American Louise Liang marries is too fine a fellow to be credible. Dr. Liang himself is much attracted to a beautiful Chinese "modern" woman, and their relationship constitutes a Hollywood motif out of keeping with the scenes in China. Yumei, James Liang's wife, is also overdrawn as an embryonic superwoman—almost always kind, patient, and self-sacrificing—a wish-fulfillment projection, too ideal to be real. Dr. Liang's own wife, a likable, often comic figure, is too consciously drawn as an earth-mother type.

In short, *Kinfolk* is a potpourri, a distinct example of the effect of trying to blend ingredients belonging to two different kinds of novels—the "serious" and the "popular."

IV   Command the Morning

Pearl Buck, fascinated by the questions raised by atomic science, traveled to Oak Ridge, Tennessee, to Los Alamos, New Mexico, and to similar atomic centers in the United States in order to learn more about the development and discoveries of modern physics. She was especially interested in interviewing scientists themselves and in obtaining their views on the bomb and on the problems stemming from nuclear science. She wrote articles, short stories, and a play about the issues involved, but her most effective creative work in this area was the novel *Command the Morning*.[18]

Command the Morning is a story of the Manhattan Project. The novel covers a period of five years during the creation, perfection, and use of the atomic bomb. The scene shifts from the University of Chicago, to Oak Ridge, and then to Los Alamos, until the explosion in the New Desert is achieved. At this point the question is whether or not the weapon should be used against Japan. When Germany was still fighting, the scientists at work on the project generally agreed that they had to produce the bomb before the Germans did. Now the issue was not so clear-cut. Germany had surrendered, and rumors had been heard that Japan was near the breaking point. Some of the scientists felt that a tight naval blockade and continued bombing with conventional weapons would bring the Japanese to surrender. The military figures, most of the American governmental officials, and a majority of the scientists felt that if the bomb were used, the war would be quickly ended and the lives of many American soldiers saved.

Throughout the novel, much soul-searching takes place, and scientist Stephen Coast has had continual misgivings about the project. He finally sides with the majority, although he regrets the necessity to use the bomb and does everything he possibly can to find an alternative solution. The woman he loves, scientist Jane Earl, protests against the bomb because she believes its use would be immoral. The will of the majority prevails: the bomb is dropped on Japan, and the scientists return to teaching or to work in industry.

Command the Morning is frankly propagandistic in purpose. Pearl Buck seems—at least at this time—to feel the way Jane Earl feels: it was immoral to drop the atomic bomb under the circumstances prevailing in 1945 and, thereby, to kill so many innocent people. Every argument against the bomb's use is marshaled. The Hungarian scientist Szigny, who has been driven from Europe by the Nazis, was a prime moving force in the original decision to make the bomb. Now he rebels against using such a weapon against the Japanese. He argues that the Japanese do not have a comparable weapon, and, hence, we do not need to fear their use of such an instrument. He states that B-29's using TNT and ordinary bombs every few days can equal the force of one A-bomb.

Another argument urged against employing the bomb is world opinion. One of the scientists asserts that Asians will believe that the United States deliberately waited until the Germans surrendered so that we would not have to test the bomb on white people. Jane Earl—who, though American, was reared in India—warns that the faith and love of the people of India for America will be seriously affected by the use of such a weapon. If "we drop the bomb we'll destroy ourselves, everywhere in the world. People won't believe in us any more,"[19] she maintains. Later she receives a letter from her former teacher in India urging her to do what she can to prevent the bomb's use. He declares that the people of the world will not forgive the United States for using it.

This novel also contends that men are ignoring the feelings and opinions of the women in the world. Jane Earl's attitude is rejected. When the usually easy-going and domestic Mollie Hall, wife of the civilian head of the project, discovers that her husband has been working on such an inhumane weapon and that it has caused such destruction in Hiroshima and Nagasaki, she becomes hysterical and regrets having had children in such a world as this. Stephen Coast's wife has been reluctant to have children under present world conditions, and even the children themselves represented by Burton Hall's teen-age son Tim are rebellious about the achievements of the scientists: "A bunch of old men plotting to kill off my generation."[20]

In its theme and in the issues with which it deals, *Command the Morning* is a thought-provoking, serious novel. On the basic question at stake, it appeals to man's conscience for the final answer. As an instructive novel, dealing with the problems of a controlled nuclear reaction and the history of the A-bomb's creation, *Command the Morning* is informative and well researched in scientific detail, almost as well documented in its way as *Arrowsmith*. Real-life scientists, such as Enrico Fermi, are mixed with fictional figures. At times, basic scientific information is fed to the reader in rather artificial ways; for example, Burton Hall attempts to explain to his uncomprehending wife how atomic energy works and some of the problems associated with it. Hall also is prone to repeat and emphasize to Jane Earl information that is clear to both of them but perhaps not to the reader.

The frequent isolation of the scientist is conveyed effectively, and the division rising between the scientist-husband and the nonscientist wife is convincingly witnessed. Buck shows considerable respect for the brilliance of science and its never-ending searches. At the end of the story the atomic bomb is, in a sense, obsolete; and the younger scientists are turning to missiles and rockets. The novel takes its title from this situation: in the Old Testament God had humbled Job by asking him if he had "commanded the morning?" When the new scientific discoveries eventually bring man to the control of space, then humankind will be able to answer this question in the affirmative.

With all of its virtues, however, *Command the Morning* is not a literary success. The didacticism is too heavy, and the propaganda pulls the story away from artistic balance. The affectionate feeling created between Stephen Coast and Jane Earl is obviously engineered solely for romantic interest and with a definite eye toward Hollywood. Above all, the novel's major weakness rests in its characterizations: the characters are simply types to illustrate various reactions and viewpoints. While in accumulation of scientific detail alone *Command the Morning* might rival *Arrowsmith*, it creates no such memorable figures as Max Gottlieb, Leora Tozer, or Dr. Pickerbaugh. V.S. Pritchett's comment on the personages in *Command the Morning* is particularly apropos. He notes "the small emotional range of Miss Buck's characters: like early Hemingway figures they merely feel 'bad' or feel 'good.' Between times they have 'problems.'"[21]

Closely related to *Command the Morning* in its concern with the morality of the atomic bomb's use is Pearl Buck's play *A Desert Incident*.[22] This drama involves scientists working on a secret governmental project at a site in the Arizona desert. When a British scientist on the project team learns that he is helping to construct a super-destructive weapon, he wants to withdraw. At the end of the play, however, the great danger of the new product is acknowledged by all, and the scientists involved decide to join in an attempt to direct atomic power into peaceful uses.

In this play Pearl Buck declares that American and British scientists should refuse to give their governments any knowledge of weapons that could be used in future wars. She holds to this belief even if Communist scientists would not agree to do the same. While such a unilateral position is extreme and highly debatable (although Buck does not consider the even touchier problem of unilateral disarmament), one critic's reaction to this idea is of interest. Kenneth Tynan, pointing out in no uncertain terms that *A Desert Incident* is a poor play, felt called upon to relate a story about a friend of his who was quite unconcerned about the possibility of world destruction in a thermonuclear holocaust. Tynan wrote: "[Pearl Buck] chose the most important subject in the world, and though she handled it vaguely and emotionally, she came down on the side of life, while the detached, historical viewpoint of my smiling friend led him to espouse the cause of death. Because of her choice, and her commitment, I am prepared to forgive Miss Buck a great deal."[23]

In order to reinforce the framework of *A Desert Incident* Pearl Buck does, for her, an unusual thing: she uses symbolism. Two cantankerous children are introduced to represent man and woman at the beginning of time, when they did not know that they had to unite for the propagation of the race.[24] An Indian servant and his wife carry on a farcical sex relationship which, according to Buck's explanation, represents a period of time when the man was not certain whether or not his offspring were legitimate. An unhappy married couple in the play symbolize man and woman in disassociation and, therefore, man and woman in torment. Elinor, the play's heroine, represents the modern woman in a world of science. Elinor works out a sound relationship with other people and adjusts to life's demands and responsibilities.

Buck's venture into symbolism is disastrous, partly because she attempts to cover too many areas of life. As Brooks Atkinson noted in his review of the play, the drama is so "overloaded with points of view that it leaves its main theme as anti-climax."[25] Further, her use of symbolism is alternately grandiose and overly simple so that a jarring incongruity results between what the symbolism intends to do and what it actually says. Her symbolism obfuscates where it should enlighten, and it is thoroughly deficient in both appropriateness and subtlety.

Pearl Buck's *A Desert Incident*, as well as her other dramas, demonstrates that her writing forte was the novel. The format of a stage play was too restricting for her talent. She needed the wide panoramic scope furnished by the novel in order to spin lengthy sagas and introduce a numerous array of characters.

CHAPTER 8

A Humanitarian As Well

ALTHOUGH she told Theodore Harris that she was not a humanitarian, Pearl Buck fits every aspect of this term. She attempted to reject the humanitarian label because she felt this appellation denigrated her written work and she thought of herself as a writer. For her, authorship was a special vocation. She stressed that her function was "to write books."[1]

Yet at least since the 1930s the designations "author and humanitarian" are too closely related to Pearl Buck to be separated. Humanitarianism concerns have been intimately related to her literary preoccupations.

Fundamental and central to her humanitarianism is Buck's lifelong and intense struggle against racial prejudice. This feeling grew from Buck's earliest childhood days, but it impressed itself on her particularly at two periods: during the Boxer Rebellion and during the Nationalist uprising of 1926–27.

Buck's parents tried as much as possible to live among the ordinary Chinese people; they eschewed mission compounds and engendered in their daughter strong feelings of charity and tolerance. When she was eight years old, her Chinese friends began to behave toward her with hostility. She noticed that her schoolmates also began acting strangely. Her mother explained that feeling against white people was running high because, in the past, people from Western countries had often mistreated and victimized the Chinese. The young girl commenced to understand that all white people were now classified as one group, even though not all of these had done injury to the Chinese. Up to this time Pearl Buck had been unaware of hatred, and she was unable to accept the fact that she, her parents, and other whites were categorized with whites who were imperialists and exploiters. Even the Chinese who favored her and her parents had to pretend coldness and aloofness so that they might remain free from censure from those who did display the old animosities. Although Pearl and her parents were innocent of any wrongdoing, they were hated because of the color of their skin, because of their race.

For the first time the young child knew fear and peril. Rumors scattered the word that Tzu Hsi, the reigning Empress Dowager, the same monarch about whom Buck would later write a novel, was determined to drive the white people out of the country. Her patience with the whites who plundered, stole, demanded special concessions and treatment, and even killed, was exhausted, and she wanted to take drastic action. Pearl Buck's father sympathized with Tzu Hsi's feelings; he acknowledged that the whites had usurped and looted parts of China and had often behaved without moral or legal obligations.

Although Absalom Sydenstricker could understand the Empress Mother's anger, he did not think it would manifest itself as it did. The first news of the slaughter in Shantung province of the missionaries and of little children was chilling indeed. Peril was no longer imminent; it had arrived. The Boxer Rebellion forced Caroline Sydenstricker and her children to flee to Shanghai. Neither father nor mother wished to go, but the news that innocent white children had been murdered was the deciding factor. Only a few belongings could be taken, and the family silver was buried in the yard. The flag at the American consulate was changed to a banner of solid red, the predetermined signal for immediate flight. Absalom Sydenstricker guided his refugee family to Shanghai and courageously returned to his mission post.

About her refugee year in Shanghai Pearl's memory is vague. One episode, however, was unforgettable. While walking along a heavily congested street, the young girl became impatient at the slow pace of a Chinese man who walked ahead of her mother and her. The Chinese gentleman had a tassel at the end of his queue. Pearl pulled this tassel very slightly, and the gentleman turned upon her in fury. Her mother apologized instantly and later warned the child of the danger of such an act. For the first time Pearl had seen her mother afraid. When the child realized that her mother was frightened of a Chinese, she knew a grave change had occurred. After the Boxer Rebellion Pearl Buck realized that her world as a white person and as an inhabitant of China, while united in many ways, must be separate to some degree— the conduct of earlier white men in China had brought about this condition.

The forced departure from her Chinese home during the Boxer Rebellion in 1900 remains engraved indelibly on Pearl Buck's mind.

But another salient impression shares itself with this initial awareness of fear and danger. In 1926–27 a new revolutionary movement occurred in China. This Nationalist-Communist uprising had a distinctive anti-foreign antagonism at its core. Her father refused to recognize or acknowledge this fact but she remembered the look of hatred on the Chinese gentleman's face when she had pulled his queue during the refugee period in Shanghai twenty-seven years previously. She also recalled the many provocations that imperialists from Western countries had given to the Chinese for many years. Although they had been warned by the American consul to leave Nanking because of the animosity of the revolutionaries, the Sydenstrickers stayed on.

In March of 1927 the Nationalist soldiers attacked Nanking, and on the morning of March 27 news was brought that the revolutionary forces, which had conquered the city, were killing whites. Dr. Williams, vice-president of the Christian university in Nanking, was one of the first white people to die. Pearl Buck and the other individuals in her household—her husband, her two children, her father, her sister, her sister's husband and child—received the shattering news of the killings and sought a place to hide. Much noise was heard in the distance, and the sounds of death came closer every moment. Almost immediately Mrs. Lu came through the back gate to offer shelter to her white friends. She guided the group to the half-room which was her home. This half-room was located in a thickly populated area of mud houses and had no window, only a hole in the roof. Through the hole they could see the sky reflecting flames from burning buildings, and Pearl's father declared that the seminary where he taught was burning. Again Pearl realized that, although she and her family had helped the Chinese and treated them kindly, the injustice of other white people was associated with her and her relatives. She and the members of her family because of their color were forced to find shelter from hatred and death.

In their congested shelter the huddled refugees could hear their own home being invaded and looted by wild, yelling mobs. Time passed slowly. All the neighbors of Mrs. Lu knew that Pearl Buck and her family were in hiding for their lives, but the people wished to protect them. Chinese friends even went to the commander-in-chief of the revolutionary forces in order to intercede for the Americans. These emissaries returned near the end of the afternoon with news that the army commander had refused to spare white people. The possibility of death came closer.

Then later the loud thunder of cannon was heard. At first the idea of cannon seemed incredible since the Chinese had none. Suddenly, the refugees knew that American and British warships in the river were shelling the area. Some time later revolutionary soldiers, directed by a Chinese friend, came to the hiding place and escorted the refugees to a university building where many white people had been taken under guard. All of these people had been saved and aided in some way by Chinese friends. The commanders of the British and American ships arranged for the release of the whites, and the refugees were taken aboard the gunboats for the trip to Shanghai. Pearl Buck remembered with great gratitude the many Chinese who risked their lives in many ways to help the white people during this crucial period. This was one of the main impressions she recalled from this whole episode. Material possessions were lost, but her feelings for people deepened; and the importance of human relationships struck an even deeper note in her heart.

Particularly as a result of her family training and her experiences during the Boxer Rebellion and the revolutionary uprising of 1926–27, Pearl Buck has always stressed the idea of humanity above all other concerns. Since she is of both the East and the West, she is sensitive to both points of view. If she saw many Chinese behaving in an extreme and hostile manner, she could understand that they were simply reacting against former injustices. In her thoughtful and appealing autobiography, *My Several Worlds*, which in itself is a warm document of humanity, she candidly admits that if she had been a young Chinese who had been instructed in the various wars, concessions, usurpations, unequal treaties, etc., which the white men carried to China, she too would have wanted to drive whites out of the country.[2] At the same time Buck notes that many, many Chinese exalted humanity and kindness above hostility, even though they were aware of past injustice. Her humane approach to people everywhere stems from such experiences and thoughts.

Buck not only denounced racial prejudice wherever she found it, but she also sought in much of her fiction and nonfiction to explain Asians to Americans and Americans to Asians in order to bring about a mutual understanding of attitudes, differences, and problems. For example, in *Friend to Friend*, a colloquy carried on with Carlos Romulo, Buck noted the Far Eastern hatred of colonialism and explained that America bitterly disappointed many Asian countries by not denouncing colonialism at every opportunity.[3]

Although several books and articles have attempted to explain to

Americans why we are not popular in Asia, much of Pearl Buck's writing on this topic antedates later commentaries by many years. If one had read her work to any degree, one would understand Asian attitudes toward the United States, and much of the bafflement of the still prevalent we-send-them-millions-of-dollars-in-aid-why-don't-they-like-us? school of thought would vanish. This enlightenment in itself—a by-product of Buck's understanding of humanity—gives her work a valuable quality of helping us to understand how we appear in the eyes of the world. On this level alone Buck's writing provides an element of insight needed by many Americans.

It is further to Pearl Buck's credit that she does not present a single-sided picture. Past and present misconduct by white men does not furnish a complete answer to present misunderstandings. She admits negativeness, caprices, and petulance among many Asians. She records, for example, that Asian countries that have previously been controlled by colonial powers are still prone to blame all their troubles on their former masters and to shirk their own responsibility for improving their lot and for developing their own leadership.

Nevertheless, despite weaknesses and crotchets on both sides, Buck believes that, in a spirit of free inquiry and increased knowledge, America and Asia can come to know and understand each other's positions, improve their relationship, and concentrate on spreading the world necessities of food, medical care, education, peace, and freedom. Much of her writing and many of her lectures and speeches have been directed to this end so that her humanitarianism often expresses itself in written form.

While her writing has considered the important worldwide questions of international cooperation and the major questions of war and peace, her interest in the individual and in more local concerns has never flagged. Several examples can be cited to support this conclusion, to demonstrate Buck's public consciousness, and to show that several of her efforts have met with success.

After the United States government closed Ellis Island in New York harbor as an Immigration Center in 1954, new immigrants to America were held in the Federal House of Detention in Manhattan and in Westchester County (New York) Jail. New arrivals to the United States, guilty of no crime, were held in these prisons—often for several months—until their records were processed. Thus, they were thrown together with criminals and limited in movement, recreational facilities, and the other ordinary amenities of life. Such treatment, guaranteed to make a mockery of the words carved on the

Statue of Liberty, caused frustration and disappointment to many of these inmates and aroused the anger of friends and relatives who visited them in their quarters. Aware of Pearl Buck's humanitarian interests, many of these people contacted her.

On November 16, 1954, she wrote a letter, which was published in the *New York Times*, protesting this practice and citing several examples of immigrants suffering under such duress.[4] The *Times* immediately adopted this cause and editorialized on the injustice and hardships involved.[5] Less than a month later, on December 10, 1954, the Immigration and Naturalization Service ceased this practice, and detained aliens were removed from federal prisons. The following day the *Times* published an editorial praising the government's action and thanked Pearl Buck for having first called attention to the problem.[6] This case is just one of many in which Buck has moved the public conscience, and it illustrates an important facet of her thought, which is reiterated frequently in her writing.

Buck's humanitarian work that has most captured the fancy of the public everywhere has been her activity on behalf of unwanted children. In 1949 she and her husband Richard Walsh founded Welcome House, an adoption agency for American-Asian children. Welcome House grew out of the problem of finding families willing to adopt children of mixed Asian-American blood. Relatively few homes were open to such children, and many institutions able to handle these boys and girls simply would not receive them. At first Pearl Buck and her husband took into their Bucks County, Pennsylvania, home a Chinese-American baby and a young Indian-American child. Interested neighbors then joined in the plan, and a house was established nearby where foster parents could care for a group of children. Originally, Welcome House was concerned with children of mixed blood who were born in America. As time went on, Welcome House began to serve as an adoption agency and attempted to bring children from overseas for adoption. Hundreds of children were fathered by American servicemen in such places as Japan, Okinawa, and Korea. In some cases their fathers and mothers have disclaimed any responsibility for their care. Since these children are half-American, they are often discriminated against in their native countries and, consequently, find themselves ostracized. These children are rootless, and in time can become a possible source of political unrest and rebellion. As Pearl Buck has pointed out, the American people have largely ignored this problem; and, while many of these boys and girls could be placed for adoption in the United

States, American laws are presently not amenable to any large-scale attempts to help these children.[7] While some of the problems involving children of mixed blood persist, Welcome House has cared for countless orphans and unwanted children and placed many in foster homes. It has attempted to help these children grow up as Americans with a pride in both their Asian and American heritage.

In 1964 the Pearl S. Buck Foundation was established. The Foundation is a nonprofit agency devoted to caring for children of half-American parentage who are forced to remain overseas. The Foundation's purposes are "(1) to educate the American public to the existence and needs of the Amerasian children and the American responsibility to them; (2) to educate the Amerasian children so that they will, when adults, be responsible, productive human beings—a credit to both sides of their ancestry; (3) to build a climate of social acceptance for these children in the countries of their birth."[8]

The Foundation furnishes medical care, clothing, counseling, and educational opportunities. The Amerasian children are not supported or aided by any formal U.S. government programs. The Pearl S. Buck Foundation is thus the only agency dedicated exclusively to assisting these children and their Asian mothers (or guardians). The Foundation carries on its work through charitable donations. In addition to funds donated by average citizens it receives royalties from several of Buck's books.

The Foundation's headquarters are now located at Green Hills Farm, Pearl Buck's former estate, in Bucks County, Pennsylvania. It supports bilingual social workers in the five countries where it maintains child assistance centers: Korea, Thailand, Taiwan, Okinawa, and the Philippines.[9]

Buck has also played a prominent role in helping mentally retarded children. Her only nonadopted child was handicapped in this manner, and Pearl Buck has described this situation and all of its implications in a book called *The Child Who Never Grew.* Over a period of many years she has written about this problem and has taken a very active role in The Training School at Vineland, New Jersey. This famous institution was originally founded in 1888 for the purposes of caring for and treating mental retardation and for training people to work with the retarded. Valuable research into the causes and treatment of this illness is also done at The Training School.

A few additional examples of Buck's humanitarian preoccupations indicate the wide range of her interests and the sensibleness of her viewpoints. In 1941 she founded the East and West Association, a nonprofit organization which attempted to bring about greater harmony and world understanding through the interchange of books, lectures, motion pictures, and radio programs. Before and during World War II, Buck was one of the active members in a group that brought much food and medical relief to China. She has also participated in various freedom movements. Long before India's freedom was achieved, she was a staunch supporter for India's independence from Great Britain and was one of the incorporators of the Mahatma Gandhi Memorial Foundation, formed to promote the humanitarian ideals of Gandhi.

It is indeed amazing that one woman could have such wide concerns and take such a vital role in all these various activities and, at the same time, carry on a writing career resulting in the production of over one hundred books. Until one possesses some knowledge of Buck's humanitarianism and understands the dominant part it plays in her thinking and writing, one cannot fully comprehend her career. A basic feeling for the importance of each individual in the world and an all-embracing realization of the fundamental unity of all men permeates her thought and work. In these two aspects she is reminiscent most of all of Walt Whitman. Together they share an overwhelming obsession with freedom and equality, an unshaken faith in the common man, and a persistent belief in progress.

Through her humanitarian practice, and through her books and magazine articles, Buck had contact with millions of Americans, especially from the 1930s to the 1960s. It appears possible that her constant emphasis on human rights, her denunciation of racial prejudice, her encouragement of women to use their minds and develop career interests, and similar theses germinated in, and penetrated into, many minds until today such views are widespread in contemporary society. Pearl Buck doubtless had some measure of influence in these developments.

CHAPTER 9

Novels of the Last Decade

IN the final ten years of her life Buck continued to take an active interest in the Pearl S. Buck Foundation and to write numerous books in several genres.[1] Her most widely read and most significant works were novels. Some, such as *Death in the Castle* (1965) and *All Under Heaven* (1973), proved exceedingly weak, but several other works of fiction are important thematically as well as artistically, and two novels of this period—*The Living Reed* and *The Time Is Noon*—rank among the most interesting of her career.

I   The Living Reed

The Living Reed, a most ambitious work, appeared in 1963. In this lengthy saga Pearl Buck traces the history of Korea and the noble Kim family, beginning in 1883 when a treaty was signed with the United States and concluding just after World War II when American forces landed at Inchon.

The narrative, divided into three parts, commences with a description of Il-han, his wife Sunia, and their two sons. Il-han is one of the monarchy's closest advisors. Buck arranges for Il-han to tour the country in order to gauge the feelings and conditions of the people. This is a rather artificial device enabling the reader to become familiar with Korea. Surveyed are the monks in their Buddhist temples in the mountains, the seafolk on the coast, and the hard-pressed peasants.

The country's political turmoil and intrigue include dissension between the King and the Queen. America does not fulfill its 1883 treaty commitment to guarantee the sovereignty of Korea; as a result, an eventual dispute between China and Japan ends with Japanese occupation. Korea becomes merely a colony of imperial Japan. The Korean language is prohibited in the schools, and only

Japanese books are allowed. Japanese brutality and oppression rage unceasingly, and, in time, Queen Min is murdered.

Yul-han, one of Il-han's sons, is killed, along with his wife and daughter, when the Japanese deliberately lock and set fire to a church filled with Christians. The Christians, constantly accused of plotting against Japanese control, are the principal target of the conquerors.

Yul-chun, Il-han's other son, becomes active in the rebel movement. He calls himself "The Living Reed" since the bamboo shoot symbolizes the ever-present spirit of independence which springs anew to take the place of broken shoots. The struggle for freedom never ceases.

When Woodrow Wilson urges self-determination for the peoples of the world, he becomes a hero to the Koreans struggling for independence. The aristocratic Il-han even visits Wilson in Paris during the Peace Conference after the First World War. (Historically a Korean delegation did meet with Wilson at that time.) Yet the Japanese oppression continues.

When the Japanese attack America in World War II, the Koreans and the independence movement gain fresh hope. They feel that the Americans will liberate them. After the war, however, the Russians, with American acquiescence, seize the northern part of the country as far as the 38th parallel. Then when the Americans do land, they turn to the Japanese usurpers for guidance while the natives are mistreated and ignored.

In a lengthy prefatory "Historical Note," Pearl Buck observes that the historical facts of the novel, including the Woodrow Wilson material, the deliberate burning of the crowded church, and the Inchon betrayal, are accurate. This provides a decidedly authentic background into which the fictional characters are worked. We observe a blending of textbook and novel, which makes the documentary material more lively. Buck also presents effective background descriptions of the cities and countryside and gives a very thorough portrayal of traditional marriage and burial customs, celebrations, and social activities.

The first two sections of the book remain the most forceful, for in these segments Il-han and Sunia arouse interest and play convincing roles. Il-han's relationship to Queen Min and his part in her flight and eventual return to the throne are attention-arousing episodes, and Il-han's other activities on behalf of his country strike a compelling note. It must be admitted, however, that often throughout the novel the characters become too subordinate to the events and documentation.

Part 2, in which Yul-han and his wife become more significant, also has both historical and character appeal. This second unit relies heavily on the Woodrow Wilson data, noting Korea's strategic importance as a desirable goal for Russia, China, and Japan, and emphasizing the absolute necessity of Korean independence from foreign control. This second part ends powerfully on a grisly note as thousands are killed during the Mansei Demonstration and many churches are intentionally burned, incinerating their congregations.

Part 3 features Yul-chun and Il-han's grandson Liang. This is the least successful segment. Yul-chun wanders as a rebel throughout China, Manchuria, and Korea, and the novel becomes choppy, episodic, largely unfocused. He never manages to capture the imagination and never genuinely comes alive. Further, Liang and his dancer girl friend seem like characters from a fairy tale. While the novel ends effectively by building up Korean expectations for the American arrival and contrasting these hopes with the brutality and insensitivity that occur, the drama of this conclusion cannot overcome the weak characterization and jumpy movement which predominates in the final unit.

Although the various characters should have been frequently rendered more vividly and the episodic quality of the novel does occasionally distract, *The Living Reed* overall presents an arresting and informative panoramic view of nineteenth- and twentieth-century Korea. Since Korea has played such a significant part in recent world and American history, the book takes on a historical and social value which has rightly made it one of the most widely read of Pearl Buck's later novels.[2]

II The Time is Noon

The most fascinatingly autobiographical novel in the last decade of Pearl Buck's career was *The Time Is Noon*, published in 1967. Significantly enough, the book was written in the late 1930s, but after being set in type it was withdrawn by her and Richard Walsh because it was believed to be too personal.[3] This personal element is very evident. Joan Richards, the book's heroine, is constantly described as very "tall," with a "big body," and having much energy and romantic idealism. She possesses a strong longing for marriage and children. Although the setting is transposed to Pennsylvania in the 1920s, Joan's father is a deeply religious, but cold and aloof, Presbyterian minister, and her mother is extremely warm, spirited, and family oriented. Although the father is respected, he does not obtain much love from his family because of his remote and totally God-centered demeanor. It is the mother who attracts and draws the family together. Affinities with Pearl Buck's own mother and father are very obvious.

When the mother becomes ill, it is Joan who tends her through the long months of a sickness that is terminal. After her mother's death, Joan remains at home and takes care of her father. When he suffers an unexpected stroke and dies, Joan is left alone. She marries a farmer, Bart Pounder, but soon finds him and his family repulsive. She (like her real-life counterpart) has a mentally retarded child by him and then refuses to have further marital relations. When he is discovered having sex with a rather pathetic farm girl, she excuses his behavior by saying that she did wrong to marry him, that they were not suitable, and that he would have been really happy with someone else—perhaps the neighboring farm girl. Joan Richards's comment here echoes in many ways a later statement Pearl Buck made about her first husband, John Lossing Buck.[4]

In time Joan falls in love with Roger Bair, a dashing aviator who, although he obviously loves Joan, feels he must stay with and support his delicate wife. It is apparent, however, that Roger will find some way to join Joan as the novel ends on a hopeful note. Again it is evident that, although several factors are altered, the Pearl Buck-Richard Walsh relationship is dominant in the novelist's mind.[5] The fact that Pearl Buck and Richard Walsh divorced their respective spouses in order to marry is too coincidental to be overlooked.

Although the novel has much autobiographical interest, it is more significant because it boasts some of the best writing of Pearl Buck's career. The description of a minister's family life in the 1920s is impressively accurate and authentic. The unearthly, God-obsessed father, whose only real concern and interest is his religious vocation, and the lively, loving, considerate mother who attempts to make the best of a situation that is extremely unpalatable to her produce a credible and intriguing conflict. The three children are also very well delineated: the energetic and romantic Joan, the irreligious and bored brother, Frank, and the deeply spiritual sister, Rose, who idolizes her father. The compromises and tensions dominating such a diverse group are described in genuine detail, and the mother's resentment when the money she has saved for years out of family expenses is demanded by the father for his missionary endeavors in South End, an impoverished black slum, implants itself deeply in the reader's mind. When she becomes deathly ill, the mother refuses to see her husband at all. She has heroically borne his lack of consideration and his ethereal remoteness during their life together, but she demands total freedom while she approaches death. Again, this situation is factual.

After the passing of her parents Joan marries and goes to live with her in-laws. The Pounder family exists only to tend their farm. Theirs is a home centered on work, Bible reading, and joylessness. Silence predominates in this household, and any deviation from the daily norm is looked upon with suspicion and hostility. Again Pearl Buck has been able to describe another household with penetrating authenticity. It is difficult to imagine any other American novelist portraying these particular scenes with greater impact. They are reminiscent of Pearl Buck at the height of her talent in the 1930s. There is a starkness, a realism, a forcefulness that would have enabled students of Buck's career to suspect that *The Time Is Noon* was written closer to the time period of *The Good Earth*, *The Exile*, *Fighting Angel*, and *The Mother* even if we did not possess Buck's autobiographical confirmation as to the date of authorship.

Yet *The Time Is Noon*, while possessing a masterfully realistic description of two households, is weakened by defects that have occurred all too often in Pearl Buck's fiction. In her Chinese storytelling mold she must overplot. It almost appears that she is telling a bedtime story in serial form. At each bedtime telling she must invent newer and newer happenings which strain credulity and force sophisticated readers to lose faith in the logic of the narrative.

Joan's sister Rose marries a missionary, and she and her husband go to labor among the Chinese in far-off Asia. They are eventually killed by bandits, but their two children are saved through the help of a friendly amah and brought to the United States. Meanwhile, brother Frank has had an illegitimate child by one of the black girls in the South End ghetto. Joan has now left her husband and his family and acquired a home of her own. She rears in happy unison her own retarded son, her brother's son, and her sister's two children. While there is a semi-Welcome House–Pearl S. Buck Foundation theme present to uplift, the improbability of all this overplotting must force any serious reader into disbelief.

This improbability of plot is further heightened by the intrusion of Roger Bair. He is added solely to give a love interest and to produce a cloying, optimistic ending. Joan Richards meets him very briefly but immediately loves him. Many pages later she sends a letter asking his help. Soon he is at her side, ready to do her bidding. It is all too pat. True, Joan finds out, to her enormous surprise, that he is married (since she is 33 years old and he a good bit older one would think it could not be much of a surprise). This plot complication is to be resolved in the future, however, presumably by the death of his frail wife.

The Time Is Noon is another propagandistic novel in the manner of so many of Buck's post-1930s books. The thesis of the need for love and caring, kindness and generosity and the optimistic belief that every cloud has a silver lining overwhelms the book and finally reduces it to a farfetched soap-opera level. The plot is frequently wrenched violently and twisted incredibly to support the message being propounded.

The novel will doubtless retain attention to the end, but any analysis must focus on the miscellany of discordant materials within the covers of one book—superb characterization and authentic realism for perhaps two hundred fifty pages and then the most improbable occurrences and unbelievable characters (e.g., Roger Bair) all melded into a rather flat "everything for the best" conclusion. This is the striking quality of so much of Buck's fiction—a quality compounded of too facile philosophizing, too quick writing with little revision, and an emphasis on the Chinese storytelling motif where almost anything appears permissible to keep the narrative moving.

III   *Other Fiction—in Brief*

While none of her post-*The Time Is Noon* novels contain as many well-wrought scenes, some of her last novels cannot fairly be ignored. *The New Year* (1968) rates a high priority among this group.

Attorney Christopher Winters is a happily married, well-to-do, up-and-coming politician. As a popular candidate for governor of Pennsylvania, he appears to be future presidential timber. While he progresses in his campaign, he receives a letter from his half-Korean son, Kim, whom he had fathered while an American serviceman twelve years previously. Kim suffers much unhappiness in Seoul because of his half-American parentage. Since he has no official father, the boy cannot go to school or even hold a regular job. Legally in Korea, the lad does not exist since in that country the father is responsible for children and must register the offspring.

When Christopher's wife, Laura, learns of her husband's Korean son (she and Chris have no children of their own), she travels to Korea to view the situation at first hand. After observing Kim's plight and seeing other half-American children in the same position, she returns to America with her stepson. Christopher places the lad in a leading New England prep school while he pursues his political ambitions. Kim, although he makes heroic attempts at adjustment, endures much loneliness and isolation. His real identity is kept secret. He has everything but a family and a home. Laura perceives his emptiness and attempts to convince her husband to formally acknowledge his son and bring him into the family. After being elected governor, Christopher accedes to Laura's wishes; and an optimistic, pleasant, but rather improbable conclusion results.

The subject of the neglected half-American children in Asia is a topic that deeply touched Pearl Buck's interest as both Welcome House and her Foundation testify. While *The New Year* does not present several episodes in convincing fashion (the Mr. Choe material, for example, which becomes a deus ex machina escape for Kim's mother Soonya), it does succeed in portraying the predicament of Kim with the utmost realism. There is a compelling sense of the social problem Kim and others like him represent. They are children of two worlds, yet in so many ways belong to neither. This issue, while obviously and patly treated in many sections of *The New Year*, achieves a starkness and contemporary impact that stings and must touch even the hardest heart.

The Three Daughters of Madame Liang (1969) is less successful in dealing with another contemporary topic—the merits of democracy versus the limits of totalitarian regimes. Madame Liang runs a thriving restaurant in Red-controlled Shanghai, although her three daughters are living in the United States, having been educated there. Two of the women return to Communist China. Grace, the eldest, a medical doctor, is at first distressed by primitive Chinese practices but eventually becomes a totally committed party member. Mercy, the second daughter, and her intellectual husband return with the enthusiastic doctrinaire goal of serving the homeland. In time they are bitterly disillusioned by Communist dogmatic narrowness and regimentation. Only the third sister, who remains in America, really achieves genuine freedom from the harsh restrictions of totalitarianism.

The problem with this novel is that the thesis becomes too obviously forced. Pearl Buck appears now too distanced from Red China to make the scene persuasive. She has obviously kept up with the latest news accounts, but there is a remote, almost fairy-tale aura surrounding the events and characters. The book reads smoothly and contains Buck's usual narrative interest, but the reader is too far removed from the characters to become more than sketchily involved. This defect is not true of Joan Richards in *The Time Is Noon* or of Kim in *The New Year*.

Again, however, few Buck novels are without rewarding insights and observations on some basic problem or issue. In *The Three Daughters of Madame Liang*, we are persuaded that various systems of philosophy and government will come and go. There will be revolutions and counterrevolutions, but China itself cannot be subjugated for long because of its vastness and huge population. Strict Communism or any other totalitarian system in China cannot, Pearl Buck argues, ultimately survive under these conditions. China's desire for beauty and the knowledge of ancestral influences cannot be stamped out. The wisdom and antiquity of countless centuries must come to dominate. As she says in a magazine interview: "China is stronger than Communism. She will make out of it what she wants."[6]

Whether one accepts this thesis or not, its argument is so cogently presented by Madame Liang and by the events that take place in the novel (including the Red Guards youth group uprisings under Mao) that once more Buck has strengthened a book by bringing readers to significant reflection.

Two more novels must be mentioned. *Mandala* (1970) was intended to be a "big novel" of India, treating that country on a grand scale. The protagonist, Maharana Prince Jagat, hopes to modernize an impressive Indian palace and develop a popular tourist hotel. His only son, Jai, is reported killed by the Chinese in a border conflict, yet his wife insists that the young man is alive. While Jagat searches for his son, he meets a beautiful, well-to-do American woman, Brooke Westley. Jagat and Brooke fall in love, but finally Brooke gives up her lover and returns to America. She realizes that he is needed by his people, and in order to retain their respect as a leader he must not separate from his wife and become permanently involved with a foreigner.

The story drives forward rapidly, and Pearl Buck's never-failing ability to plot—frequently overplot—never flags. Further narrative interest occurs when Jagat's daughter veers between attraction for an Indian and a bustling American businessman. The spiritual motif, so strong in Indian saga, is also not ignored. A reincarnation theme becomes pronounced, and Jagat's son seemingly appears at the end of the story; he has been born anew as a young boy in a small village.

Although Pearl Buck has visited India, she does not capture the authenticity of the scene or make her characters consistently credible. Despite its ennobling themes—the power and eternality of love, the desire for self-sacrifice, and the value and need for spirituality—the novel becomes inundated by overplotting and soap-opera qualities.

Pearl Buck gave much thought to writing a love triangle of a middle-aged woman whose male admirers would be much older and younger. This novel, *The Goddess Abides*, was published in 1972.

Edith Chardman is a wealthy, intellectual, and still attractive forty-two-year-old widow. She has a beautiful townhouse in Philadelphia and a pleasant home in Vermont. She meets twenty-four-year-old Jared Barnow, a physicist who has brilliant talents and goals. His work also combines studies in biology and engineering. He helps invent instruments and techniques to assist amputees and other handicapped individuals achieve feeling in their cineplastic limbs.

Edith's other admirer is a seventy-six-year-old philosopher named Edwin Steadley. At every opportunity he enthusiastically declares his love and applauds the inspiration she gives him. It is her love that sustains his life, and he insists that he could not continue writing his memoirs and even face death fearlessly unless this love was paramount.

Her love begins to convince Steadley that death is not final. Edith's husband, an obvious portrait of Richard Walsh, did not believe in the immortality of the soul. It was one of the few points on which Walsh and Pearl Buck differed. She did not really come to a definitive conclusion, but she left open the door of possibility. Edwin Steadley, who is based on retired Harvard philosopher Ernest Hocking, looks upon survival after death as a moral imperative. The spirit and the love closely united with it possess unique power, a force that must reunite even beyond the grave. When in the course of time Steadley realizes that death is near, he writes Edith a final letter emphasizing their reunion in a spiritual form.

After the death of Steadley, Edith turns with more attention to the young scientist. The real-life counterpart of Jared Barnow is unknown, although certainly some of the qualities of youth and admiration may be based upon Theodore Harris, Pearl Buck's official biographer.

As the relationship develops, the same aspects that aided and buoyed the philosopher Steadley affect Barnow. Such statements as "Love gives life to the lover as well as to the beloved"[7] and "Love keeps me not only living but alive" are illustrated and reiterated by the relationship.[8]

Edith Chardman eventually refuses Jared's marriage proposal. She feels that she is too old for him, could not conceive children at her age, and that she herself is now too independent to live on a close, day-to-day husband-wife basis. She does support his relationship with, and eventual marriage to, a girl his own age who is worthy of his character and capabilities.

Jared will, however, continue to worship Edith. He regards her as a goddess; and she, according to the mystique of the goddess, becomes even more of a goddess by giving him up. "She must set herself apart if she was to fulfill the monumental task, which in itself must be perfection."[9]

At the beginning of the book there is a quotation from Robert Graves's *The White Goddess* which reinforces the concept of woman's needed role as goddess and the salutary effects this brings to herself and those around her. Uncertainty remains as to how autobiographical this is in Pearl Buck's own case, but certainly this is a theory to which she subscribes and urges women to achieve. She does not probe deeply into the concept. There is no analysis of primitive goddesses or other in-depth study or research. She does believe that a woman can rise to heights of spiritual development and inspiration, and in so doing becomes glorified in herself and as a model for others. Much of this thinking derives from Ernest Hocking. In one of his letters to her he emphasizes her goddess role in his own life. He feels that she inspires him with her love and presence and raises him to a heavenly plane. He regards such a goddess as more significant to the human race than any father-god.[10]

Although the theme of woman's power and glory and the concept of self-sacrifice and inspiration arouses interest and evokes fascination, *The Goddess Abides* is not persuasive. Both Jared Barnow and Edwin Steadley appear too idealistic and too other-worldly. They seem to be exaggerating their devotion, constantly attitudinizing. Their feelings for Edith Chardman frequently are farfetched and maudlin. And yet a reading of several of Ernest Hocking's love letters to Pearl Buck produces the same effect.[11] Comparing Theodore Harris's obvious adoration expressed in *For Spacious Skies* pushes one to the conclusion that Pearl Buck was the object of such effusive, seemingly excessive emotional outpouring. Although such glorification did take place in real life, her attempt to transmit this in fictional form is unduly sentimental and exaggerated.

In the last decade of her career, as well as posthumously, several collections of Pearl Buck's short stories have been published. As of 1980 her publishers have in their possession twenty-six more short stories and one novella, most of which will be issued in future editions.

Buck's short stories, except for some of her early period narratives, add little to her literary reputation.[12] Their interest is mainly autobiographical. In "The Woman Who Was Changed," for example, a happily married couple is rent asunder when the wife becomes a successful author. The wife, intrigued by her creations, "making people come to life," ultimately finds this vocation "to mean more than anything."

Nevertheless, the occasional autobiographical touches do not outweigh the narrative deficiencies.[13] Pearl Buck's short fiction is comprised mainly of what used to be called women's magazine stories. The tales are smooth and readable, but usually sentimental, improbable, and simplistic in approach. They lack the strength, penetration, realism, and thematic significance that distinguished *The Good Earth*, her biographies, and some of her early novels.

CHAPTER 10

A Final Reckoning

I N presenting a summation of the career of Pearl Buck, some evalu-
ation of her literary status must be established. Although she has
been ignored by many critics and not accepted by the literary
establishment, it may be maintained with much justification that she
has written at least three books of undoubted significance: *The Good
Earth* and the biographies of her father and mother. Certainly, *The
Good Earth* is a masterpiece that will be remembered by subsequent
generations as a work that powerfully and movingly describes a
whole way of life.

I *Early Career Aspects*

Many attempts have been made to explain away *The Good Earth*'s
popularity by assigning rather facile theories. For instance, it has
been a commonplace of much literary criticism, and has been
reiterated in some of Buck's obituary notices, that *The Good Earth*
achieved success because of the common theme of poverty and social
injustice during the Depression and the book's concomitant uplifting
message at that time.[1] Yet nearly fifty years later *The Good Earth*
continues to be studied in most high schools and several colleges and
widely read throughout the world.

The two Nobel Prize biographies are among the most deeply felt
and penetrating analyses in any literature of the missionary caught in
an alien climate, the demands of the missionary life, and the
concomitant reaction to such demands. While Andrew Sydenstricker
exemplifies the essence of the drive and intensity of the nineteenth-
century missionary spirit, his wife Carie symbolizes the perennial
demands of humanity for a more compromising balance between
earthly and spiritual goals.

Several of Buck's other books—particularly *Sons*, *The Mother*,
The Patriot, and *The Time Is Noon*—contain many effective

segments. Although they do not achieve the heights they sought, they do contain many notable sections and several compelling episodes.

At about the time of the Nobel Award—after the completion of *The Patriot*—Pearl Buck's writing career certainly seemed to be in the ascent, and to promise further important achievement. After this period, however, Buck's humanitarian preoccupations increased. These interests, carried into her fiction, immediately weakened the objectivity of her creation. She began to assert didactic considerations to such an excessive degree that novels such as *Dragon Seed* and *The Promise* became propaganda efforts on behalf of China's struggle against Japan. No longer could James Joyce's famous dictum be applied about the objectivity of the artist, "The artist . . . remains within or behind or beyond or above his handiwork, invisible, refined, out of existence, indifferent, paring his fingernails," although his comment would pertain perfectly to *The Good Earth*.

After 1939 she became more facile at constructing her plots, handling dialogue, and in the technical aspects of her craft; but no subsequent significant growth in the artistic features of novel writing occurred in Pearl Buck's work. No experimentation in technique took place, and she made no attempt to penetrate more deeply into character analysis, showed no willingness to seek subtleties of tone or mood, and indicated no interest in using myth or symbolism or other elements characteristic of the modern novel. On this account alone, Buck must be neglected by some of the more recent literary critics because her total disregard of such concerns as myth and archetype, stream-of-consciousness, and symbolism gives critics relatively little to analyze and explicate. Her novels do not furnish the layers of meaning and the complexity that modern literary criticism demands.

The reason Buck refused to keep pace with modern techniques is not far to seek. She followed the old-fashioned Chinese story practice of emphasizing event and characterization. And yet there is a dichotomy even here. In the 1930s her best fiction was objective, and the didactic element was usually muted or subordinated. When written in this vein, her work took on force and meaning. After 1939, however, she broke away from objectivity; didacticism became a dominant feature, and the quality of her work declined. If she had followed the same form of imitation of the Chinese novel type in her post-Nobel Prize writing, her work after 1939 might have reached the significance of her earlier productions. Increasing humanitarian interests brought a lack of vraisemblance and demonstrated the inadvisability of distorting what Thomas Hardy calls "natural truth" for the purpose of making didactic points. A growing sentimentalism also made itself felt more and more in her later writing, and this attitude was detrimental to the highest artistry. It is notable that *The Time Is Noon* (issued in 1967), perhaps her most searingly realistic novel published since the 1930s, was written between 1936 and 1939.[2]

It can be admitted that her later work, while it does not approach her early writing, was often saved from mere best-seller ephemera by her interest in vital subjects and in humanitarian themes. In *Other Gods, Command the Morning, The New Year,* and similar novels, the reader is often rewarded by the posing and consideration of issues and problems of the utmost importance. In *The Hidden Flower* not only are the difficulties of an interracial marriage considered, but the question of a state anti-miscegenation law and its effects are examined. Many states did enforce laws banning marriages not only between Caucasians and Negroes, but between Caucasians and others of mixed blood. Some state laws, for example, specifically mentioned Mongolians, Hindus, and Indians. The irrationality and injustice of such laws are evident, and yet such regulations did exist and were enforced in almost half of the fifty American states. This is the sort of timely and distressing problem that Buck so often either tackled directly or shed some light on in her post-Nobel Prize writing. Thus the reading of most of Buck's fiction almost always involves something more than a well-told, entertaining story. Her books offer thoughtful and provocative insights into some of the most challenging issues mankind has faced and continues to face. It is this quality, generally overlooked by critics, that gives value to her later work. Elizabeth Janeway's remarks on this point deserve mention for they indicate why many intelligent readers find Buck's writing of considerable interest:

Her readership is secure. She has something to say and says it with lucid ease. If she lacks the warmth of humor she makes up for it by the warmth of sympathy. If she has a mission she can also tell a story. She writes consistently and successfully to be read; . . . it is too bad that Miss Buck's audience is, par excellence, the audience which is ignored by contemporary critics of writing. This audience is the American middle-class woman who reads novels. Thirty years ago H. L. Mencken may have been right in seeing her as an idiot who took her attention from her house, her children, and her servants only to gossip about her neighbors. She is not an idiot today.

If our mores are changing in the direction of tolerance, if our knowledge of the world is broadening, it is she who is accepting the change. It is vital to communicate with this woman, for if literature has first of all the duty of reflecting life truly (I don't mean photographically), it has the second duty of presenting this reflection to as large an audience as possible. For twenty years Miss Buck has done this. It is an excellent thing that she continues to do it so well.[3]

While Mrs. Janeway's remarks refer to Pearl Buck's creative writing, much the same thing could be said of her work in the area of nonfiction. In her essays on the "medieval" and on the "gunpowder" women, in her writing on retarded children, on adoption practices, etc., Buck has had an indisputable influence on American womanhood, much more deeply than most of us would realize or even consider. By her own participation in the Pearl S. Buck Foundation, Welcome House, in the East and West Association, etc., Buck reenforced her writing with the implementation of theoretical improvement and humanitarianism.

II *Critical Reactions*

In addition to her refusal to adopt more modern techniques in her handling of the novel and her post-Nobel Prize obsession with didacticism, several other factors are involved in her lack of popularity with the more influential literary critics. For one thing her work suffered from the inevitable critical reaction against her best-seller status.

Best-selling popular writers arouse envy, especially from those who had hoped to achieve larger audiences and more attention. An example of this reaction can be viewed in an obituary essay written for the *New Republic* by Helen F. Snow. Snow asserts that the Chinese Communists object to Buck's glorification of the old Confucian family system and the upper classes.[4] Whether Pearl Buck really "glorifies" these aspects is begging the question, but Snow is very sympathetic to the Communist view of Buck. Snow further denigrates Buck's writing as untrue to Chinese life, an accusation that harks back to the Younghill Kang's 1933 attack, and a charge that has long since been refuted.[5] Snow even goes so far as to claim that *The Good Earth* was successful only because it was packaged by an astute merchandiser, Richard Walsh, and contained a strong sexual element. Helen Snow's antagonism is due to her political views which cause her to distort facts.

Certainly, too, the fact that Buck is a woman author did not help her standing with the literari. She herself once remarked on this matter:

"Women artists in any field are not taken as seriously as men, however serious their work. It is true that they often achieve high popular success. But this counts against them as artists."[6] In this same context Buck noted that American critics sometimes praise European women artists, but they find it difficult to admit that the American variety can really be artistic. Now outdated by the "women's movement" of the 1970s, this charge could be supported by perusing earlier critical studies. Herbert Muller's condescending attitude toward women writers and his general "damning with faint praise" approach in his *Modern Fiction* immediately come to mind.[7]

Another factor in Pearl Buck's loss of prestige in serious literary circles stems from her optimistic, affirmative point of view. She did not lose her faith in progress, and she exalted a Rousseau-Thomas Paine, Transcendental type of belief in the basic goodness of humanity. On the other hand, bleak pessimism, subjective studies of anguish, and searing indictments of humanity are very much the fashion at the moment. Our Age of Anxiety appears attuned to a Samuel Beckett mood, and with such bleak tendencies Buck was *deliberately* out of step.[8] She was not an escapist; she saw and understood the evils, pressures, and problems of the present era. From time to time in her personal life she experienced more than her share of poverty, peril, disappointment, and heartbreak. But she possessed an affirmative, positive, optimistic, and idealistic temperament, and she tried to put forward the more hopeful aspects of the human situation.[9] In *American Argument* she spoke of contemporary young novelists who "write books of futility and despair," and she asserted that in their work "there is no vision, even though this is the most exciting age in human history, when the people of the whole world for the first time move with a common impulse toward a better life. Our young men and women look only at themselves and so see nothing."[10]

Many years ago in an important magazine article, "The Artist in a World of Science," she expressed her faith in the power of science to build a marvelous new life if men would work toward brotherhood and toward the one-world concept.[11] The potential power of scientific discoveries should bring men to a state of optimism, and the disciplined artist should work from the framework of hope while he searches life and mankind for explanations of existence. She asserted that the artist must not indulge himself in pessimism or despair. He should rather emphasize faith in the future and faith in man to improve life and the conditions of life. While acknowledging the dramatic power of John Osborne's *Look Back in Anger*, she found it deficient in point of view because it suggests a regression to animalism. Such an attitude, she argued, leads to defeat and death, while the material of the artist is life.

It is perhaps difficult not to admire Pearl S. Buck as a person. Any thoughtful and fair-minded individual must also admire the things she stands for, her viewpoints, and her humanitarianism.[12] Once, in *American Argument*, she admitted the truth of the following statement about herself, "I am always in love with great ends."[13] This comment is the best revelation she has given us of her mind and soul. It epitomizes her humanitarianism—in both thought and action— and is the key to her nature.

With all due admiration for Pearl Buck's humanitarian interests, one can at the same time wish that she had not written so much. Yet she had a compulsion to write, write, write, a *furor scribendi*.[14] Even when money was not required she could not stop the flow of her pen. Writing was an obsession ("a pressure" within herself, she called it), and she did not have the temperament or patience to check and control the flood. If she had taken more time to think out, polish, and revise many of her novels, they would probably have been vastly improved productions. One wishes, further, that she had handled her post-Nobel Prize work with greater artistry.[15] What is truly tragic in a close perusal of the corpus of her work is that, if Buck had been reared with a higher regard for the function of the novel, she would have—in her later fiction—settled for something more than important themes combined with narrative ability. Certainly the mind was there and so too, one feels, was the talent.

Of course Pearl Buck followed the old-fashioned technique of Chinese novel writing which emphasized storytelling. Yet, as John L. Bishop has pointed out in a discussion of traditional Chinese fiction, Western novels explore much more deeply the minds of the characters than do colloquial Chinese works, resulting in more detailed and well-rounded characterization.[16] In addition to superficial and type characters, the Chinese school of novel writing led to farfetched episodes and improbable occurrences, thus inhibiting a novel from reaching the highest levels of artistry and persuasion.

Yet judged by her own standards—"to please and to amuse . . . to entertain"—Pearl Buck must be granted considerable success.[17] She was a born storyteller who wrote page-turner books and, at the same time, brought important social, historical, and thematic issues to the forefront.

Notes and References

Chapter One

1. Pearl Buck, *All Under Heaven* (New York: Day, 1973), p. 199.
2. Pearl Buck, *My Several Worlds* (New York: Day, 1954), p. 51.
3. Ibid., p. 57.
4. Pearl Buck and Carlos Romulo, *Friend to Friend* (New York: Day, 1958), p. 126.
5. Curiously, a difference of opinion exists as to her exact age when she was taken to China. Views range from three to five months. Buck herself says three months in *American Unity and Asia* (New York: Day, 1942), p. 50, and in *What America Means to Me* (New York: Day, 1943), p. 196. Richard J. Walsh says four months in his brief biography prefaced to *The First Wife and Other Stories* (New York: Day, 1933), p. 12. Cornelia Spencer says five months, *The Exile's Daughter, A Biography of Pearl S. Buck* (New York: Coward-McCann, 1944), p. 11. Buck's publishers, asked to clarify the discrepancy, wrote that Cornelia Spencer, Buck's sister, "is likely to be more accurate on dates than other sources." The publishers note that Pearl Buck herself is not "much concerned with dates and chronology"; quoted from an undated personal communication from the John Day Company to the present writer. The house in West Virginia where Pearl Buck was born has been restored and is a tourist attraction; cf. Betsy Jordan Edgar, *Our House* (Parsons, W. V.: McClain Printing Co., 1965). See also "Pearl Buck's Own Good Earth," *Modern Maturity*, February-March 1978, pp. 50–51.
6. *My Several Worlds*, p. 62.
7. Pearl Buck has described the influence of this woman on her life in "The Old Chinese Nurse," *Fortnightly Review*, NS131 (June 1932), 757–70. This article was also printed in *The Country Gentleman*, 102 (June 1932), 14–15, 36.
8. *My Several Worlds*, p. 75.
9. Ibid.
10. Pearl Buck, "A Debt to Dickens," *Saturday Review of Literature*, April 4, 1936, pp. 11, 20, 25.
11. The best biographical sources for Pearl Buck's life in China are *My Several Worlds* and Cornelia Spencer's *The Exile's Daughter*.
12. *Hearst's International combined with Cosmopolitan*, July 1933, p. 4.
13. A classmate of Pearl Buck's at Randolph-Macon has written an interesting account of Pearl's college days: Emma Edmunds White, "Pearl S.

155

156   PEARL S. BUCK

Buck," *Randolph-Macon Woman's College Alumnae Bulletin*, 32 (February 1939), 4–12. Some additional impressions of Buck's college life may be found in two messages published in the same alumnae bulletin: "Pearl S. Buck's Message to New York Chapter," 38, No. 3 (1935), 16–17, and "Message to Randolph-Macon," 36 (September 1943), 15–16. The Randolph-Macon Woman's College Library has a collection of letters written to Buck by famous individuals.

14. *My Several Worlds*, p. 146.

15. Compare Pearl Buck, "Chinese Student Mind," *Nation*, Oct. 8, 1924, pp. 358–61.

16. *My Several Worlds*, p. 77.

17. S. J. Woolf, "Pearl Buck Finds That East and West Do Meet," *New York Times*, Nov. 20, 1938, Sect. 7, pp. 4, 19.

18. *New York Herald Tribune*, June 29, 1938, p. 11. In the light of Buck's admiration for Dreiser, it is interesting to note that when his publisher suggested that a brief biography be written about him to stimulate interest in the publication of *The Bulwark*, Dreiser suggested, in May, 1942, that he would recommend John Steinbeck, Pearl Buck, or Sinclair Lewis for the task. *Letters of Theodore Dreiser*, ed. Robert H. Elias (Philadelphia: University of Pennsylvania Press, 1959), III, 958.

19. Cornelia Spencer and Emma White furnish valuable data on Pearl Buck's life during the 1920s.

20. She has written movingly of this young girl in *The Child Who Never Grew* (New York: Day, 1950).

21. A similar occurrence in real life and the problem in general is discussed in Olga Lang's sociological study, *Chinese Family and Society* (New Haven: Yale University Press, 1946), p. 202.

22. She describes the composition and publication history of her first book in "The Writing of *East Wind: West Wind*," *The Colophon*, New York (December 1932), Part 12, No. 6, pp. 1–4.

Chapter Two

1. The history of the book's reception is traced in a special epilogue to the standard edition of *The Good Earth* (New York: Day, 1949), pp. 315–23.

2. *My Several Worlds*, p. 128.

3. The dramatization of Pearl Buck's novel was made by Owen Davis and Donald Davis, and the play was produced by The Theatre Guild in New York City on October 17, 1932. A transcript is filed in the Theatre Collection of the New York Public Library.

4. A copy of the screenplay, written by Talbot Jennings, Tess Slesinger, and Claudine West, may be found in *Twenty Best Film Plays*, ed. John Gassner (New York: Crown Publishers, 1943), pp. 875–950.

5. She has written a particularly warm tribute to the Chinese peasant and has expressed her faith in the common people in the introduction to the standard edition of *The Good Earth*, pp. v–xvi.

6. Compare *My Several Worlds*, p. 255.

7. *The Good Earth*, standard ed., p. viii.

8. Pearl Buck, "The Revolutionist," *Asia*, 28 (September 1928), 685–89, 752–56. Later published in *The First Wife and Other Stories* (New York: Day, 1933) and called "Wang Lung," pp. 201–25.

9. J. Donald Adams, *The Shape of Books to Come* (New York: Viking, 1944), p. 125.

10. *Proceedings of the American Academy of Arts and Letters and the National Institute of Arts and Letters*, Second Series, No. 3 (New York: American Academy of Arts and Letters, 1953), p. 22.

11. James Gray, *On Second Thought* (Minneapolis: University of Minnesota Press, 1946), p. 33.

12. Adams, p. 125.

13. Carl Van Doren, *The American Novel 1789–1939*, rev. ed. (New York: Macmillan, 1940), p. 353.

14. A brief but crisp appreciation of some of the effective qualities of *The Good Earth* appears in Joseph Warren Beach, *The Twentieth Century Novel* (New York: Appleton-Century-Crofts, 1932), p. 233.

15. Pearl Buck, "Advice to Unborn Novelists," *Saturday Review of Literature*, March 2, 1935, p. 520.

16. Ibid.

17. S. J. Woolf, "Pearl Buck Talks of Her Life in China," *China Weekly Review*, Sept. 24, 1932, pp. 145–46.

18. Van Doren, p. 353.

19. Phyllis Bentley, "The Art of Pearl S. Buck," *English Journal*, 24 (December 1935), 794.

20. Alexander Cowie, *The Rise of the American Novel* (New York: American Book Co., 1948), p. 748.

21. Cowie, p. 751.

22. Bentley, p. 798.

23. Oscar Cargill, *Intellectual America: Ideas on the March* (New York: Macmillan, 1941), p. 149, hereafter cited as Cargill.

24. Ibid.

25. William Lyon Phelps, *Autobiography With Letters* (New York: Oxford University Press, 1939), p. 912.

26. James D. Hart, *The Popular Book* (New York: Oxford University Press, 1950), p. 253.

27. Ibid.

28. Henry Seidel Canby, "*The Good Earth*: Pearl Buck and Nobel Prize," *Saturday Review of Literature*, Nov. 19, 1938, p. 8, hereafter cited as Canby.

29. Cargill, p. 148.

30. In an undated personal communication to the present writer from the John Day Company.

31. A reading comparing *La Terre* and *The Good Earth* readily confirms this.

32. Spencer, *The Exile's Daughter*, p. 175, hereafter cited as Spencer.

33. Buck, *My Several Worlds*, p. 19.

34. Ibid., p. 53. See also her statements in *I Believe*, ed. Clifton Fadiman (New York: Simon and Schuster, 1939), pp. 33–42, in which she affirms the freedom of the will and human initiative.

35. Van Wyck Brooks, *The Writer in America* (New York: Dutton, 1953), p. 187.

36. Buck, *My Several Worlds*, p. 317.

Chapter Three

1. Buck, *My Several Worlds*, p. 78.

2. Younghill Kang, *New Republic*, July 1, 1931, p. 185.

3. Ibid.

4. Ibid.

5. Ibid.

6. The editorial board of the magazine felt obliged to append a qualifying note about Kang's review, *New Republic*, July 1, 1931, p. 186.

7. Kiang Kang-Hu, "A Chinese Scholar's View of Mrs. Buck's Novels," *New York Times*, Jan. 15, 1933, Sect. 5, pp. 2, 16. That this attitude among Chinese intellectuals has perhaps not vanished is suggested by the only reference made to Pearl Buck in C.T. Hsia, *A History of Chinese Fiction 1917–1957* (New Haven: Yale University Press, 1961). Hsia's reference to *Imperial Woman* is slighting; moreover, it also seizes on a novel hardly representative of Buck's best work.

8. Pearl Buck, "Mrs. Buck Replies to Her Chinese Critic," *New York Times*, Jan. 15, 1933, Sect. 5, pp. 2, 19. This essay was also published as an introduction in the first Modern Library edition of *The Good Earth*.

9. *New York Times*, Jan. 16, 1933, p. 14. This editorial is conveniently available in *My Several Worlds*, pp. 281–82.

10. Pearl Buck, "China and the Foreign Chinese," *Yale Review*, 21 (Spring 1932), 539–47.

11. Buck, *My Several Worlds*, p. 239.

12. Ibid., pp. 393–94.

13. Ibid.

14. Ibid., pp. 146–47.

15. Ibid., pp. 282–83.

16. *The Good Earth*, standard ed., p. 319. R. P. Jean Tong's M.A. thesis entitled "The China of Pearl Buck," University of Montreal, 1953, also affirms the authenticity of Buck's work. It is interesting to note that the *China Weekly Review* praised *The Good Earth* for bringing out a better understanding of the basic Chinese problem—that of the farmer. "Pearl Buck Wins Coveted Nobel Prize," *China Weekly Review*, June 11, 1932, p. 41. See also Theodore F. Harris, *Pearl S. Buck. A Biography* (New York: Day, 1969), I, 139–40, hereafter cited as Harris.

17. Pearl Buck, "The Laymen's Mission Report," *The Christian Century*, Nov. 23, 1932, pp. 1434–37.

18. This pamphlet entitled "The Laymen's Mission Report" lists no publisher or place of publication but is dated 1932.

19. Pearl Buck, "Is There a Case for Foreign Missions?" *Harper's*, January 1933, pp. 143–55.

20. Buck, *Is There a Case for Foreign Missions?* (New York: Day, 1932).

21. Ibid., p. 8.

22. Buck, "Advice to Unborn Novelists," *Saturday Review of Literature*, March 2, 1935, pp. 513–14.

23. Buck, "Advice," p. 513.

24. Buck, *Is There a Case for Foreign Missions?*, Day edition, p. 30.

25. See, for example, *Newsweek*, April 22, 1933, p. 26.

26. *New York Times*, May 2, 1933, p. 15. The *New York Times Index* for 1933 indicates several news stories on this question.

27. Pearl Buck, "Easter 1933," *Cosmopolitan*, May 1933, pp. 16–17, 169.

28. *New York Times*, April 9, 1933, Sect. 2, p. 1.

29. Buck, *My Several Worlds*, p. 51.

30. *New York Times*, Sept. 25, 1932, Sect. 5, p. 1.

31. Buck gave her translation of *Shui Hu Chuan* the title *All Men Are Brothers*. This version was first published in 1933 in a two-volume edition. A revised edition was issued in 1937 in one volume. The Limited Editions Club brought out a two-volume edition of Buck's translation in 1948 with an introduction by Lin Yutang, and the Grove Press also published *All Men Are Brothers* (New York, 1957). In his study of *Shui Hu Chuan*, Richard Irwin praises Pearl Buck's translation as the best available for Western readers. He notes that her version contains minor errors, is written in too literal a style, and that the dialogue is not so idiomatic as it might be; but, in general, he applauds her rendition. Richard Gregg Irwin, *The Evolution of a Chinese Novel: Shui-hu-chuan* (Cambridge, Mass.: Harvard University Press, 1953).

32. Buck, *My Several Worlds*, pp. 148–49.

33. Ibid., p. 177.

34. *New York Times*, Oct. 29, 1932. This story was killed in the second edition and is, therefore, not listed in the *New York Times Index*. The article, however, is filed under the Pearl Buck material in the *Times* news morgue.

35. Spencer, p. 172.

36. Pearl Buck, "Chinese War Lords," *Saturday Evening Post*, April 22, 1933, pp. 3–5, 76–77.

37. Pearl Buck, *Sons* (New York: Day, 1932), p. 465.

38. Ibid., p. 385.

39. Ibid., p. 466.

40. Ibid.

41. Pearl Buck, *A House Divided* (New York: Reynal and Hitchcock, 1935), pp. 12–13. The manuscript of *A House Divided* is in the Baker Library of Dartmouth College.

42. Malcolm Cowley, "Wang Lung's Children," *New Republic*, May 10, 1939, p. 24, hereafter cited as Cowley.

43. Ibid.

44. Pearl Buck, *The Mother* (New York: Day, 1934), p. 58.

45. Ibid., p. 212.

46. Buck, *My Several Worlds*, pp. 255–56.

47. Buck discusses the prototype of the chief character in *The Mother* in *My Several Worlds*, pp. 221–23.

Chapter Four

1. An example of the Nobel-Prize-for-one-book belief is found in J. Donald Adams, "Speaking of Books," *New York Times*, Sept. 22, 1963, Sect. 7, p. 2. There is one other incorrect notion which, likewise, should be debunked; the belief that the Nobel award was in recognition of bringing about sympathetic understanding of Asians by Western readers. This concept is often found even in the most respected reference works, for example, in *The Literature of the American People*, ed. Arthur Hobson Quinn, et al. (New York: Appleton-Century-Crofts, 1951), p. 840.

2. *New York Times*, Dec. 24, 1938, p. 13.

3. Spencer, p. 191.

4. Buck, *My Several Worlds*, pp. 161–62.

5. Pearl Buck, *The Exile* (New York: Day, 1936), p. 73.

6. Ibid., p. 76. Some of the dying words of Pearl Buck's mother are exactly those spoken by Wang Lung. Compare *The Exile*, p. 75; *Sons*, p. 7.

7. Buck, *The Exile*, p. 168.

8. Ibid., p. 309.

9. Buck, *My Several Worlds*, p. 110.

10. Her father was the first person to translate the New Testament from Greek to Chinese. He also wrote a book on Chinese idioms. Hayes Jacobs, "Pearl S. Buck," *Writer's Yearbook 1963*, No. 34, p. 41.

11. Related in *Fighting Angel* (New York: Reynal and Hitchcock, 1936), pp. 242–47.

12. These comments occur in a letter from Pearl Buck to Ida Tarbell, April 29, 1934. This letter is in the collection of Ida M. Tarbell manuscripts at Allegheny College Library. A total of five Pearl Buck letters to Miss Tarbell forms part of this collection.

13. Buck, *The Exile*, p. 313.

14. The typescript of the "In Memoriam" essay is among the William Lyon Phelps collection of letters and manuscripts at the Yale University Library. This library has a large collection of Buck letters.

15. Buck, *Fighting Angel*, p. 65.

16. Ibid., p. 99.

17. Ibid., p. 36.

18. Buck, *My Several Worlds*, p. 99, 258.

19. Buck, *Fighting Angel*, p. 209.

20. Stephen Vincent and Rosemary Benét, "Two-World Success Story: Pearl Buck," *New York Herald Tribune*, Jan. 18, 1942, Sect. 9, p. 5.

21. Buck, *Fighting Angel*, p. 75.

22. Canby, p. 8.

Chapter Five

1. See Buck, *My Several Worlds*, pp. 263–65, 291; Harris, I, 82, 101–102, 112–114, 170–72.

2. Pearl Buck, *Now and Forever*, serialized in *Woman's Home Companion* (October 1936–March 1937). This novel was never published in book form. *China Gold*, a novel of wartime China, was serialized in *Collier's* February 7, 1942–April 18, 1942; like *Now and Forever*, it never appeared in book form.

3. Pearl Buck, *A Bridge for Passing* (New York: Day, 1962), p. 147.

4. This undated letter from Pearl Buck to William Lyon Phelps is deposited in the Phelps correspondence at Yale University. One of Buck's letters to Dr. Phelps not in the Yale collection is printed in his *Autobiography with Letters* (1939; rpt. New York: AMS Press, 1977), pp. 912–913.

5. Harris, I, pp. 210–12.

6. *The Young Revolutionist* (New York: Day, 1932) written at the request of the Christian Missionary Movement and sheer propaganda. That Buck came to regard this book as marginal can be seen by a comment made in Spencer's biography *The Exile's Daughter*, p. 174. Buck's publishers listed *The Young Revolutionist* as a juvenile.

7. *Nobel: The Man and His Prizes*. Ed. Nobel Foundation (Norman: University of Oklahoma Press, 1951), p. 127.

8. *Literary History of the United States*. Ed. Robert E. Spiller et al. (New York: Macmillan, 1948), II, 1383.

9. Ibid., p. 1384.

10. A good idea of Buck's popularity in Sweden from 1932 to 1944 may be garnered from the list of her books published there and the number of editions printed. Also helpful are the lists of library holdings and circulation of her books in various Swedish libraries as of 1951; see Carl L. Anderson, *The Swedish Acceptance of American Literature* (Stockholm: Almqvist and Wiksell, 1957), pp. 113–14, 149, 153.

11. The preface of *Shui Hu Chuan* may be found in *All Men Are Brothers* (New York: Day, 1933), Buck's translation of this novel.

12. *New York Times*, Nov. 23, 1938, p. 18.

13. Buck, *My Several Worlds*, p. 78.

14. During the political and intellectual ferment in the 1920s and 1930s, many Chinese intellectuals, greatly influenced by Western literature, came to regard novel writing as no longer a frivolous occupation, *My Several Worlds*, p. 127.

15. Buck, *My Several Worlds*, p. 76.

16. Canby, p. 8. The November 11, 1938 issue of the *New York Times* contains an editorial "Nobel Prize Winner," which discusses Buck's achievement, p. 24. This editorial was reprinted in the *Randolph-Macon Woman's College Alumnae Bulletin*, February 1939, pp. 2–3.

17. Cowley, p. 24.

18. Ibid.

19. Cargill, p. 154.

20. Buck, *East and West and the Novel: Sources of the Early Chinese Novel* (Peiping: North China Union Language School-California College in China, 1932).

21. Ibid., p. 15.

22. Pearl S. Buck, "On the Writing of Novels," *Randolph-Macon Woman's College Alumnae Bulletin*, June 1933, pp. 3–10.

23. Later published in book form, *The Chinese Novel* (New York: Day, 1939).

24. Buck, *The Chinese Novel*, p. 31.

25. Ibid., p. 24.

26. Ibid., pp. 58–59.

27. Lewis Gannett, "Books and Things," *New York Herald Tribune*, Aug. 5, 1939, p. 9.

28. Spencer, p. 193. One feels that at times Buck has come to mistake humanitarian and didactic values for artistic worth. She once wrote to the *New York Times* protesting an unfavorable review of Lillian Smith's *Killers of the Dream* (New York: Norton, 1978). She felt that this book was an important analysis of racial prejudice and should be read by all Americans. It should therefore, she concludes, have been given a sympathetic review, *New York Times*, Dec. 4, 1949, Sect. 7, p. 59.

29. Spencer, p. 194.

30. Ibid., p. 197.

31. Pearl Buck, "America's Medieval Women," *Harper's*, Aug. 1938, pp. 225–32; "America's Gunpowder Women," *Harper's*, July 1939, pp. 126–35. These two themes are expressed in somewhat different form in *Of Men and Women* (New York: Day, 1941).

32. Buck, *Of Men and Women*, p. 78.

33. Ibid., p. 88.

34. Ibid.

35. Ibid., p. 152.

36. These views are qualified later in *American Argument* (New York: Day, 1949).

37. Buck, *Of Men and Women*, see especially pp. 138–43.

38. Pearl Buck, *Dragon Seed* (New York: Day, 1942), p. 198.

39. Buck, *Of Men and Women*, pp. 187–88.

40. Pearl Buck, "Changing Relationships Between Men and Women," *American Women: The Changing Image*, ed. Beverly Benner Cassara (Boston: Beacon Press, 1962), pp. 3–10. This essay may be found in a slightly different form entitled "Wanted: Real Women," *Good Housekeeping*, April 1962, pp. 67, 241–44.

41. Buck, *Of Men and Women* (New York: Day, 1971), pp. 202–10.

Chapter Six

1. Pearl Buck, *The Patriot* (New York: Day, 1939), p. 14.

2. Ibid., p. 211.

3. Ibid., p. 325.

4. Pearl Buck, *Other Gods* (New York: Day, 1940), p. 381.

5. Ibid., unnumbered preface page.

6. Ibid., p. 349.

7. The best account of Buck's wartime activities is found in Henry Lee, "Pearl S. Buck—Spiritual Descendant of Tom Paine," *Saturday Review of Literature*, Dec. 5, 1942, pp. 16–18.

8. The most accessible of Buck's radio scripts are "China to America" in *Free World Theatre*, ed. Arch Oboler and Stephen Longstreet (New York: Random House, 1944), pp. 140–50, and "Will This Earth Hold?" in *Radio Drama in Action*, ed. Erik Barnouw (New York: Farrar and Rinehart, 1945), pp. 17–30. Several of Buck's radio plays appeared in *Asia* magazine. See Lucille S. Zinn, "The Works of Pearl S. Buck: A Bibliography," *Bulletin of Bibliography*, 36 (October–December 1979), 204–5.

9. Lee, p. 16.

10. Pearl Buck, "Tinder for Tomorrow," *Asia*, March 1942, pp. 153–55. This article was the basis for a speech given in New York City, February 10, 1942 and is anthologized in Pearl Buck's *American Unity and Asia* (New York: Day, 1942), pp. 22–33.

11. Buck, *American Unity and Asia*, p. 27.

12. Ibid., pp. 43–62.

13. Pearl Buck, *What America Means to Me* (New York: Day, 1943), p. 110.

14. Buck, *American Unity and Asia*, p. 113.

15. Ibid., p. 118.

16. Ibid., p. 119.

17. In another article she quotes the governor of Alabama, who had protested against a government contract because it called for nondiscriminatory practices in laboring conditions, "Freedom," *What America Means to Me*, pp. 43–44.

18. Buck, *American Unity and Asia*, pp. 96–104.

19. For Buck's most significant comments on the question of India, see *American Unity and Asia*, pp. 56–62, 74–95, and *What America Means to Me*, pp. 51–66, 154–80.

20. Pearl Buck, Lin Yutang, et al. *Freedom for India Now!* (New York: Post War World Council, 1942).

21. Buck, *What America Means to Me*, p. 132.

22. See especially *American Unity and Asia*, pp. 124–40.

23. Buck, *What America Means to Me*, p. 131.

24. Pearl Buck, *The Story of Dragon Seed* (New York: Day, 1944).

25. Even the similarity of first names suggests this comparison. Madame Chiang Kai-shek's first name was Mei-ling.

26. Buck, *Dragon Seed*, p. 86.

27. Pearl Buck, *The Promise* (New York: Day, 1943), p. 202.

28. Buck, *What America Means to Me*, p. 120.

164 PEARL S. BUCK

29. Edmund Wilson, *Classics and Commercials* (New York: Farrar, Straus, 1950), p. 132.

30. Buck, *The Promise*, p. 222.

Chapter Seven

1. Both *This Proud Heart* and *Other Gods* are serious efforts, while *Now and Forever* and *China Gold*, in which some scenes are set in America, are potboilers.

2. Pearl Buck, *American Triptych* (New York: Day, 1958), p. viii.

3. Information supplied in an undated personal communication to the present writer by Buck's publishers.

4. Buck, *American Triptych*, p. viii.

5. Only one reviewer of the novel seemingly surmised that Buck might have been connected with the book. This was Francis Hackett; see "A Sketch: Pearl Buck," *New York Herald Tribune*, Sept. 16, 1963, Book Week, p. 5.

6. Buck, *American Triptych*, p. vii.

7. Ibid., p. 185. See also Harris, I, 97.

8. Ibid., p. 244.

9. Ibid., p. 290.

10. Ibid., p. 345.

11. Ernest E. Leisy, *The American Historical Novel* (Norman: University of Oklahoma Press, 1950), p. 205.

12. Pearl Buck, *Pavilion of Women* (New York: Day, 1956), p. 270.

13. Buck, *My Several Worlds*, p. 256.

14. Buck, *A Bridge for Passing*. See especially pp. 76–77, 183–84, 254–56, and *Mrs. Stoner and the Sea, and Other Works* (New York: Ace, 1976), pp. 160–170.

15. Pearl Buck, *Kinfolk* (New York: Day, 1949), p. 303.

16. Ibid., p. 392.

17. Ibid., p. 358.

18. See the foreword to the typescript of *A Desert Incident*, p. 1. A copy of this play may be found in the Theatre Collection of the New York Public Library. See also "The Bomb—Did We Have to Drop It?" *American Weekly*, March 15, 1959, pp. 10–11, 16.

19. Pearl Buck, *Command the Morning* (New York: Day, 1959), p. 276.

20. Ibid., p. 142.

21. V. S. Pritchett's review of *Command the Morning*, *Scientific American*, July 1959, pp. 159–60, 162, 164.

22. *A Desert Incident*, earlier called *The White Bird* and *Three Against Time*, was produced at the John Golden Theatre in New York City, March 24, 1959. The reviews were uniformly poor, and the play ran only seven performances. At least four other plays by Buck reached Broadway. Her drama *The First Wife* was performed in English by a Chinese group on November 27, 1945 at the Barbizon-Plaza Theatre. Twelve performances were given. The play was developed from material in Buck's short story of the

same title. A review of *The First Wife* appeared in George Jean Nathan, *Theatre Book of the Year 1945-46* (New York: Knopf, 1946), p. 203. Buck was coauthor with Charles K. Peck, Jr. of a Broadway musical *Christine*, produced on April 28, 1960. This musical, with songs by Sammy Fain and Paul Francis Webster, was based on Hilda Wernher's novel *My Indian Family* (New York: Day, 1945). The typescripts of two of Pearl Buck's unpublished plays (*The Empress* and *Flight Into China*) are in the Theatre Collection of the New York Public Library. *The Empress* was written about 1937 but never produced. It was eventually developed into the novel *Imperial Woman*. *Flight Into China* was produced at the Paper Mill Playhouse, Millburn, N.J., September 11, 1939; it was later expanded into the novel *Peony*. She also adapted N.K. Narayan's novel *The Guide* (New York: Viking, 1958), which was first produced at the Lincoln Art Theatre, New York, in 1965. A one-act play *Sun Yat-sen* was published, but there is no performance record: *Asia*, April 1944, pp. 170-74; New York: Universal Distributors, and London: China Campaign Committee, n. d. (1944?). See also footnote 3, Chap. 2.

23. Kenneth Tynan, *Curtains* (New York: Atheneum, 1961), p. 316.

24. Buck herself explains the meaning of her symbolism in a foreword found in the typescript of the play, p. 2.

25. Brooks Atkinson, review of *A Desert Incident*, *New York Times*, March 25, 1959, p. 40.

Chapter Eight

1. Harris, I, 190.
2. Buck, *My Several Worlds*, p. 208.
3. Buck and Romulo, *Friend to Friend*, p. 83.
4. *New York Times*, Nov. 16, 1954, p. 28.
5. *New York Times*, Nov. 18, 1954, p. 32.
6. *New York Times*, Dec. 11, 1954, p. 12.
7. *New York Times*, June 9, 1957, Sect. 4, p. 10.
8. *The New Children-The Amerasians* (Perkasie, Pa.: Pearl S. Buck Foundation, n.d.): a pamphlet published by the Pearl S. Buck Foundation from their Green Hills Farm, Bucks County, headquarters.
9. *Green Hills Farm: An Historic Site* (Perkasie, Pa.: Pearl S. Buck Foundation, Inc., n.d.), a pamphlet from the Foundation's Bucks County headquarters.

Chapter Nine

1. It is a tribute to Buck's dedication to her Foundation and to the value of its purposes that the organization survived scandalous charges which brought about Theodore F. Harris's resignation as President and Executive Director, cf. "Crumbling Foundation," *Time*, July 25, 1969, p. 60. See also "Pearl Buck's Will Is Upset by Jury," *New York Times*, July 27, 1974, p. 27; November 11, 1979, Sect. 1, p. 53.

2. Since American troops are still present in South Korea, *The Living Reed* has special historical interest.

3. Pearl S. Buck, in collaboration with Theodore F. Harris, *For Spacious Skies: Journey in Dialogue* (New York: Day, 1966), pp. 191–92. Harris says *The Time Is Noon* was written from 1936 through 1939, Harris, *Pearl S. Buck*, I, 270.

4. Harris, I, 170.

5. Richard Walsh's wife, like Roger Bair's, was also a delicate individual; cf. Harris, I, 154.

6. "Interview by Dale McConathy," *Vogue*, June 1972, p. 148.

7. Pearl Buck, *The Goddess Abides* (New York: Day, 1972), p. 204.

8. Ibid., p. 205.

9. Ibid., pp. 249–50.

10. Harris, I, 353.

11. Several of Hocking's letters are printed in the first volume of the Harris biography, pp. 352–58. Irwin Block also presents some important insights ino the Buck-Hocking relationship, *The Lives of Pearl Buck* (New York: Crowell, 1973), pp. 156–59.

12. The most complete analysis of Buck's short stories appears in Paul A. Doyle, "Pearl S. Buck's Short Stories: A Survey," *English Journal*, 55 (January 1966), 62–68.

13. Lore Dickstein offers some interesting observations on autobiographical aspects in Buck's writing, "Posthumous Stories," *New York Times Book Review*, March 11, 1979, pp. 20–21. Dickstein's remarks drew a rebuke from Robert W. Bohl of the Pearl S. Buck Foundation, and Dickstein responded, *New York Times Book Review*, April 29, 1979, Sect. 7, p. 69.

Chapter Ten

1. See, for example, *Time*, March 19, 1973, p. 81.

2. Harris, I, 270.

3. Elizabeth Janeway, "The Optimistic World of Miss Buck," *New York Times*, May 25, 1952, Sect. 7, p. 4.

4. Helen F. Snow, "Pearl S. Buck 1892–1973: An Island in Time," *New Republic*, March 24, 1973, pp. 28–29.

5. See Chapter 3 of this book.

6. Buck, *Of Men and Women*, p. 67.

7. Herbert J. Muller, *Modern Fiction: A Study of Values* (New York: Funk and Wagnalls, 1937). See especially pp. 324–28.

8. Elizabeth Janeway notes this point in her review-article on Pearl Buck. In part Mrs. Janeway says: "Miss Buck's virtues are those least likely to appeal to contemporary critics; her faults must seem to them too obvious and too uninteresting to attack. She prefers to deal in human situations as close to universality as possible at a time when the private struggle of a human mind with its interior world is a favorite subject. She subordinates her characters to her theme and approximates them, often, to types. Above all, in an

intellectual world which has plunged itself into profound pessimism . . . Miss Buck is an optimist,' Janeway, p. 4.

9. Pearl Buck usually gives the impression that the majority of people are good; the Claggarts and the predatory types compose a relatively small percentage of the population. In her last years, however, she modified her views about people being born good, honest, and naturally loving. See *Mrs. Stoner and the Sea, and Other Works*, pp. 156–57.

10. Buck, *American Argument*, p. 201.

11. Pearl Buck, "The Artist in a World of Science," *Saturday Review*, Sept. 20, 1958, pp. 15–16, 42–44.

12. Or, as James Gray puts it in his *On Second Thought*, her "passionate moral concern with ideas and profound human values," p. 35.

13. Buck, *American Argument*, p. 203.

14. Harris, I, 294–95.

15. Especially distressing is her post-1939 emphasis on literature as a vehicle for teaching. In her 1933 Alumnae Address at Randolph-Macon Woman's College, she noted that the true artist should not be a preacher. As time went on, she was, unfortunately, attracted more and more to didacticism by her interest in humanitarianism and by her growing desire to influence the largest possible audience. She thus came to reject her earlier viewpoint that life—not the novelist—should do the teaching.

16. John L. Bishop, "Some Limitations of Chinese Fiction," *Far Eastern Quarterly*, 15 (February 1956), 239–47.

17. Charles Poore's comments are realistic. He asserts that "she chooses wortny subjects to write about . . . is an accomplished craftsman when it comes to putting a novel together . . . and keeps her story going with lively incidents," "Books of the Times," *New York Times*, April 24, 1949, p. 23.

Selected Bibliography

PRIMARY SOURCES

This is an accurate listing of Buck's most significant books published in English, which corrects several publication date errors in Harris's bibliography, Harris, I, 367–72. Some books have date discrepancies because they were copyrighted in one year but published the following year. See also the Chronology at the beginning of this book as well as the Zinn checklist.

1. Novels and Short Story Collections

East Wind: West Wind. New York: Day, 1930.

The Good Earth. New York: Day, 1931.

Sons. New York: Day, 1932.

The First Wife and Other Stories. New York: Day, 1933.

The Mother. New York: Day, 1934.

A House Divided. New York: Reynal and Hitchcock, 1935.

House of Earth (trilogy of *The Good Earth, Sons, A House Divided*). New York: Reynal and Hitchcock, 1935.

This Proud Heart. New York: Reynal and Hitchcock, 1938.

The Patriot. New York: Day, 1939.

Other Gods: An American Legend. New York: Day, 1940.

Today and Forever: Stories of China. New York: Day, 1941.

China Sky. Philadelphia: Triangle, 1942.

Dragon Seed. New York: Day, 1942.

The Promise. New York: Day, 1943.

China Flight. Philadelphia: Triangle, 1945.

Portrait of a Marriage. New York: Day, 1945.

The Townsman (as John Sedges). New York: Day, 1945.

Pavilion of Women. New York: Day, 1946.

The Angry Wife (as John Sedges). New York: Day, 1947.

Far and Near: Stories of Japan, China and America. New York: Day, 1947.

Peony. New York: Day, 1948.

Kinfolk. New York: Day, 1949.

The Long Love (as John Sedges). New York: Day, 1949.

God's Men. New York: Day, 1951.

The Hidden Flower. New York: Day, 1952.

Bright Procession (as John Sedges). New York: Day, 1952.

Voices in the House (as John Sedges). New York: Day, 1953.

Come, My Beloved. New York: Day, 1953.

Imperial Woman. New York: Day, 1956.

Letter from Peking. New York: Day, 1957.

Command the Morning. New York: Day, 1959.

Fourteen Stories. New York: Day, 1961.

Satan Never Sleeps. New York: Pocket Books, 1962.

Hearts Come Home and Other Stories. New York: Pocket Books, 1962.

The Living Reed. New York: Day, 1963.

Stories of China. New York: Day, 1964.

Death in the Castle. New York: Day, 1965.

The Time Is Noon. New York: Day, 1967.

The New Year. New York: Day, 1968.

The Three Daughters of Madame Liang. New York: Day, 1969.

The Good Deed and Other Stories of Asia, Past and Present. New York: Day, 1969.

Mandala. New York: Day, 1970.

The Goddess Abides. New York: Day, 1972.

All Under Heaven. New York: Day, 1973.

The Rainbow. New York: Day, 1974.

East and West. New York: Day, 1975.

Mrs. Stoner and the Sea, and Other Works. New York: Ace, 1976. This paperback contains nine short stories and three new essays, including "What I Believe," and "What I Wish for America." All twelve items copyrighted in the 1970s. *Secrets of the Heart.* New York: Day, 1976.

The Lovers and Other Stories. New York: Day, 1977.

The Woman Who Was Changed and Other Stories. New York: Crowell, 1979.

2. General Fiction and Nonfiction (including the most significant pamphlets)

The Young Revolutionist (juvenile). New York: Day, 1932.

Is There a Case for Foreign Missions? New York: Day, 1932.

East and West and the Novel: Sources of the Early Chinese Novel. Peking: North China Union Language School–California College in China, 1932.

All Men Are Brothers (translation of *Shui Hu Chuan*). New York: Day, 1933.

The Exile. New York: Reynal and Hitchcock, 1936.

Fighting Angel. New York: Reynal and Hitchcock, 1936.

The Chinese Novel. New York: Day, 1939.

Stories for Little Children. New York: Day, 1940.

Of Men and Women. New York: Day, 1941 [Reissued in 1971 with a new epilogue].

American Unity and Asia. New York: Day, 1942.

Pearl Buck Speaks for Democracy. New York: Common Council for American Unity, 1942.

The Chinese Children Next Door (juvenile). New York: Day, 1942.

The Water Buffalo Children (juvenile). New York: Day, 1943.

What America Means to Me. New York: Day, 1943.

The Spirit and the Flesh (*The Exile* and *Fighting Angel* in one volume). New York: Day, 1944.

The Story of Dragon Seed. New York: Day, 1944.

The Dragon Fish (juvenile). New York: Day, 1944.

Tell the People: Talks with James Yen about the Mass Education Movement. New York: Day, 1945.

Yu Lan: Flying Boy of China (juvenile). New York: Day, 1945.

Talk about Russia, with Masha Scott. New York: Day, 1945.

China in Black and White: An Album of Woodcuts by Contemporary Chinese Artists (editor). New York: Day, 1945.

How It Happens: Talk about the German People, 1914–1933 (in collaboration with Erna von Pustau). New York: Day, 1947.

The Big Wave (juvenile). New York: Day, 1948.

American Argument (in collaboration with Eslanda Goode Robeson). New York: Day, 1949.

The Child Who Never Grew. New York: Day, 1950.

One Bright Day (juvenile). New York: Day, 1950.

The Man Who Changed China: The Story of Sun Yat Sen (juvenile). New York: Random House, 1953.

Johnny Jack and His Beginnings (juvenile). New York: Day, 1954.

My Several Worlds. New York: Day, 1954.

The Beech Tree (juvenile). New York: Day, 1955.

Christmas Miniature (juvenile). New York: Day, 1957.

Friend to Friend (in collaboration with Carlos Romulo). New York: Day, 1958.

The Delights of Learning. Pittsburgh: University of Pittsburgh Press, 1960.

The Christmas Ghost (juvenile). New York: Day, 1960.

A Bridge for Passing. New York: Day, 1962.

Welcome Child (juvenile). New York: Day, 1964.

The Joy of Children. New York: Day, 1964.

Fairy Tales of the Orient (editor). New York: Simon & Schuster, 1965.

Children for Adoption. New York: Random House, 1965.

The Gifts They Bring: Our Debt to the Mentally Retarded (in collaboration with Gweneth T. Zarfoss). New York: Day, 1965.

The Big Fight (juvenile). New York: Day, 1965.

My Mother's House (in collaboration with others). Richwood, West Virginia: Appalachian Press, 1965.

For Spacious Skies: Journey in Dialogue (in collaboration with Theodore F. Harris). New York: Day, 1966.

Essay on Myself and *A Study of Pearl S. Buck* by Jason Lindsey. New York: Day, 1966.

The People of Japan. New York: Simon & Schuster, 1966.

The Little Fox in the Middle (juvenile). New York: Macmillan (Collier Books), 1966.

To My Daughters, With Love. New York: Day, 1967.

Matthew, Mark, Luke, and John (juvenile). New York: Day, 1967.

Elements of Democracy in the Chinese Traditional Culture. Jamaica, New York: Center of Asian Studies, St. John's University, 1969.

The Kennedy Women: A Personal Approach. New York: Cowles-Day, 1970.

China as I See It (edited by Theodore F. Harris). New York: Day, 1970.

The Story Bible. New York: Bartholomew House, 1971.

The Chinese Story Teller (juvenile). New York: Day, 1971.

Pearl Buck's America. New York: Bartholomew House, 1971.

China: Past and Present. New York: Day, 1972.

A Community Success Story (in collaboration with Elisabeth Waechter). New York: Day, 1972.

Once Upon a Christmas. New York: Day, 1972.

Pearl Buck's Oriental Cookbook. New York: Simon & Schuster, 1972.

A Gift for the Children (juvenile). New York: Day, 1973.

Mrs. Starling's Problem (juvenile). New York: Day, 1973.

Words of Love. New York: Day, 1974.

Pearl S. Buck's Book of Christmas (editor). New York: Simon & Schuster, 1974.

SECONDARY SOURCES

BARNES, ANNE. "They Have Their Exits." *TLS*, November 5, 1976, p. 1405. A review of *The Rainbow* which emphasizes the melodrama of Buck's last novel and the wooden quality of the characters.

BARTLETT, ROBERT M. "East and West—One World: Pearl S. Buck," in *They Work for Tomorrow.* New York: Association Press and Fleming H. Revell, 1943, pp. 32-40. Stresses the need for the Western and Asiatic people to become acquainted with each other and see their common goals and needs.

BENTLEY, PHYLLIS. "The Art of Pearl S. Buck." *English Journal*, 24 (December 1935), 791-800. A pioneering, perceptive, and appreciative study of Pearl Buck's handling of scene, style, characterization, plot, and theme.

BIRMINGHAM, FREDERIC A. "Pearl Buck and The Good Earth of Vermont." *Saturday Evening Post*, Spring 1972, 70-73, 135, 139, 141, 143-44. Visits Buck in Vermont and interviews her. Discusses how she helped restore the beauty and economy of Danby, Vermont; presents a laudatory analysis of her stately and kindly character; and gives a

172 PEARL S. BUCK

commentary on her philosophy of life and various literary, humanitarian activities.

BLOCK, IRWIN. *The Lives of Pearl Buck*. New York: Thomas Y. Crowell Co., 1973. Written for young adults, this volume gives a good brief exposition of biography basics and highlights. It is especially informative about Buck's relationship with her husbands and with Ernest Hocking.

BRENNI, VITO. "Pearl Buck: A Selected Bibliography." *Bulletin of Bibliography*, 22 (May–August 1957), 65–69; (September–December, 1957), 94–96. Particularly helpful checklist of Buck's articles in periodicals and edited collections up to 1955. Superseded by Zinn's checklist.

CANBY, HENRY SEIDEL. "*The Good Earth*: Pearl Buck and the Nobel Prize." *Saturday Review of Literature*, November 19, 1938, 8. Brief, succinct, and balanced essay on the pros and cons of the awarding of the Nobel Prize to Pearl Buck.

CARGILL, OSCAR. *Intellectual America: Ideas on the March*. New York: Macmillan, 1941; New York: Cooper Square Publishers, 1968, pp. 146–54. Considers Buck's relationship to the Naturalists.

CARRASCAL, JOSÉ MARÍA. "Pearl S. Buck a sus setenta y siete años," *La Estafeta Literaria*, No. 432, November 15, 1969, pp. 14–15. Buck's popularity is due to her clear style and exotic themes.

CARSON, E. H. A. "Pearl Buck's Chinese." *Canadian Bookman*, 21 (June–July 1939), 55–59. Provocative, balanced account of Pearl Buck's career up to 1939.

CEVASCO, GEORGE A. "Pearl Buck and the Chinese Novel." *Asian Studies*, 5 (December 1967), 437–50. A perceptive analysis of the characteristics of Buck's Chinese fiction. Believes that novels like *The Good Earth*, *The Mother*, *Dragon Seed*, and *The Patriot* will always retain their appeal.

———. "Reviews." *Chinese Culture*, 6 (October 1965), 107–09. A review-essay praising Doàn-Cao-Lý's book. Believes that this volume is very helpful in giving readers a more intimate understanding of Buck's characters and the world she portrays.

COOPER, ALICE C. and CHARLES A. PALMER. "Pearl S. Buck: East Meets West," in *Twenty Modern Americans*. New York: Harcourt, Brace, 1942, pp. 291–307. Deals almost exclusively with biographical details.

COURNOS, JOHN and SYBIL NORTON. "Pearl Sydenstricker Buck—Interpreter of the East," in *Famous Modern American Novelists*. New York: Dodd, Mead and Co. 1952, pp. 85–91. Focuses on biographical data; contains no significant literary criticism.

COWLEY, MALCOLM. "Wang Lung's Children." *New Republic*, May 10, 1939, 24–25. A review-article primarily concerned with *The Patriot* but discussing most of Pearl Buck's work.

DICKSTEIN, LORE. "Posthumous Stories." *New York Times Book Review*, March 11, 1979, Sect. 7, pp. 20–21. Buck is part of the history of China because she chronicles the era from the old dynasty to the modern state and made China live for American readers. Maintains that she is more interesting as a person than as a writer.

DOÀN-CAO-LÝ. *The Image of the Chinese Family in Pearl Buck's Novels.* Saigon: Dúc-Sinh, 1964. Emphasizes Buck's firsthand knowledge of Chinese settings and the authenticity of her scenic and character portrayals. Observes that the Chinese women are portrayed as superior to the men.

DOYLE, PAUL A. "Pearl S. Buck's Short Stories: A Survey." *English Journal,* 55 (January 1966), 62–68. Some of Buck's early narratives such as "The First Wife," "The Angel," and "Enough for a Lifetime" are effective examples of old-fashioned, traditional storytelling, but most of her short stories are too facile, improbable, and simplistic.

HARRIS, THEODORE F. *Pearl S. Buck. A Biography.* New York: Day, 1969, 1971. These two volumes written "in consultation with Pearl S. Buck" are, along with her autobiography *My Several Worlds,* the main sources of necessary biographical data. Volume 2 consists entirely of a selected number of her speeches, essays, and letters chosen to convey her philosophy.

HENCHOZ, AMI. "A Permanent Element in Pearl Buck's Novels." *English Studies,* 25 (August 1943), 97–103. A thoughtful article which analyzes Buck's use of conflict and contrast to develop the themes of pain, sacrifice, and innocent victims.

HOYLMAN, ALTA. "Pearl Buck's Own Good Earth." *Modern Maturity,* February–March 1978, pp. 50–51. Discusses Stulting Place, the West Virginia family home where Buck was born. The homestead has been attractively restored and is maintained as a tourist attraction.

LANGLOIS, WALTER G. "*The Dream of the Red Chamber, The Good Earth,* and *Man's Fate*: Chronicles of Social Change in China." *Literature East and West,* 11 (March 1967), 1–10. *The Good Earth* is socially important because it describes the agricultural masses of the Middle Kingdom during the years when outside forces began to impinge on this group.

LASK, THOMAS. "A Missionary Heritage." *New York Times,* March 7, 1973, p. 40. Buck possessed an excellent awareness of, and sympathy for, all aspects of humanity. She wanted a wide audience to hear her humanitarian messages, which were developed from her missionary upbringing. Other than *The Good Earth* and her biographies, her books are too "facile" and "slack."

LEE, HENRY. "Pearl S. Buck—Spiritual Descendant of Tom Paine." *Saturday Review of Literature,* Dec. 5, 1942, 16–18. A report on the wartime activities of Pearl Buck, with emphasis on some of her various humanitarian endeavors.

LINDSEY, JASON. *A Study of Pearl S. Buck.* New York: Day, 1966. This was published as the second part of a pamphlet co-entitled *Essay on Myself* by Pearl S. Buck. Lindsey gives an excessively eulogistic commentary on her literary career, emphasizing the reasons why she deserves the Nobel

Prize. He believes she is one of America's greatest writers.

"Notes on Current Books." *Virginia Quarterly Review*, Spring 1976, 59–60. Praises the variety of stories in the *East and West* collection. Stresses that Buck understands character complexities and has considerable sympathy for these complexities.

"Pearl Buck." *New York Times*, March 7, 1973, p. 42. This editorial praises Buck for her humanitarianism and for conveying the reality of China to her readers. Her winning the Nobel Prize may be justified for the same reasons that Winston Churchill won the award. "It was a testament to the breadth of her vision and the greatness of her human spirit." The *Times* devoted considerable space to Buck's death and burial; see the obituary notice by Albin Krebs, March 7, 1973, pp. 1, 40, and also March 10, 1973, p. 34.

SHIMIZU, MAMORU. "On Some Stylistic Features, Chiefly Biblical, of *The Good Earth*." *Studies in English Literature* (Tokyo), English Number 1964, pp. 117–34. Demonstrates, with numerous examples, how biblical style has deeply influenced *The Good Earth* and become an integral part of the novel.

SINHA, SIMITA. "The Novels of Pearl S. Buck—A Study in Major Themes." Diss. Lucknow University, India, 1974. Buck's works treat significant subject matter and are often stylistically effective. Her emphasis on faith and optimism is valuable in a negative era, yet she lacks a deeply philosophic mind and a Camus-like intellect. Buck has a Victorian reserve in handling sexual material. Her novels of other countries do not help the reader to understand native people's special racial characteristics because she stresses common traits shared with all humankind.

SNOW, HELEN F. "Pearl S. Buck 1892–1973: An Island in Time." *New Republic*, March 24, 1973, 28–29. Deprecates Buck's writing as an untrue portrayal of Chinese life. Claims that Buck glorifies the upper classes and that *The Good Earth* was successful only because of its sexual element and effective merchandising by her publisher.

SPENCER, CORNELIA. *The Exile's Daughter, A Biography of Pearl S. Buck*. New York: Coward-McCann, 1944. This biographical study was written by Pearl Buck's sister. Although at times it puts too much emphasis on household, garden, and other marginal details, this work is very thorough on biographical facts about Pearl Buck's childhood, her life in China, and her Randolph-Macon College years. This very useful biography carries us to the World War II period. Contains no literary criticism except a little eulogizing here and there. Cornelia Spencer is a pseudonym for Grace S. Yaukey.

THOMPSON, DODY WESTON. "Pearl Buck," in *American Winners of the Nobel Literary Prize*. Ed. Warren G. French and Walter E. Kidd. Norman: University of Oklahoma Press, 1968, pp. 85–110. Interesting survey of some of Buck's strengths and weaknesses. Feels that Buck's writing appeals to idealists, to students whose hopes and ideals have not yet been disillusioned by experience.

VAN DOREN, CARL. *The American Novel 1789-1939*. Rev. ed. New York: Macmillan, 1940, pp. 350-53. Praises the style and richness of *The Good Earth*.

VAN GELDER, ROBERT. *Writers and Writing*. New York: Scribner's, 1946. Brief but informative revelation of some of Buck's writing habits.

WALSH, RICHARD J. *A Biographical Sketch of Pearl S. Buck*. New York: Day, Reynal and Hitchcock, 1936. This is essentially the same essay found in Walsh's "Introduction" to *The First Wife and Other Stories*; however, the data has been expanded and a useful bibliography of Buck's early writing is included.

WOOLF, S. J. "Pearl Buck Talks of Her Life in China." *China Weekly Review*, Sept. 24, 1932, 145-46. Valuable in establishing the style influences on Pearl Buck's writing—the King James version of the Bible and the old Chinese sagas.

ZINN, LUCILLE S. "The Works of Pearl S. Buck: A Bibliography." *Bulletin of Bibliography*, 36 (October–December 1979), 194-208. Superseding the Brenni checklist, this is the most complete listing of primary and secondary material yet compiled. It is a superlative work of research. Lucille Zinn is associated with the Pearl S. Buck Birthplace Foundation, Inc., which operates Buck's ancestral home in West Virginia as a museum and owns most of Buck's manuscripts.

Index

Aeneid, 114
American Academy of Arts and Letters, 31
Arrowsmith, 126–27
Asia magazine, 30
Atkinson, Brooks, 128
Atlantic Monthly, 22

Balzac, Honoré de, 40
Beals, Victor, 19
Beckett, Samuel, 152
Benét, Rosemary, 74
Benét, Stephen Vincent, 74
Bentley, Phyllis, 34–35
Bishop, John L., 153
Boxer Rebellion, 70, 73, 129, 130, 132
Brecht, Bertolt, 64–65
Brooks, Van Wyck, 40
Buck, Carol, 22
Buck, John Lossing, 20–21, 77, 140
Buck, Pearl S.: early years, 16–23, 129–32, 155n5, 155n 13; estimate of literary significance, 32–33, 67, 74–76, 80–83, 148–53; the foreign missions controversy, 46–49; her literary theories, 84–88, 108, 148–51, 153, 167n15; humanitarianism, 101–106, 120–21, 132–36; the John Sedges novels, 113–17; medieval and gunpowder women, 88–90, 92–93; Naturalism, 38–41, 109–10; Nobel Prize, 29, 67, 80–83, 85–87, 148–49, 153; portrait of China attacked and defended, 42–46, 122, 151; World War II activities, 101–106; writing for radio, 102, 163n8; playwriting, 127–28, 156n3, 164n22

WORKS: FICTION
All Under Heaven, 137
Angry Wife, The, 113, 117

Bright Procession, 91, 113, 117
"China and the West," 23
China Gold, 121
"Chinese Woman Speaks, A," 23
Command the Morning, 124–27, 150
Death in the Castle, 137
Desert Incident, A, 127–28
Dragon Seed, 91, 106–10, 112, 149
East Wind: West Wind, 23–28, 37, 44, 80, 120
Goddess Abides, The, 145
Good Earth, The, 26, 28, 29–45, 50, 51, 53, 55–56, 62, 65, 67, 83, 109, 110, 116, 120, 122, 141, 147, 148, 149, 151
Hidden Flower, The, 150
House Divided, A, 50, 56–61, 109, 121
House of Earth trilogy, 50, 59, 62, 80, 97
Kinfolk, 121–24
Living Reed, The, 137–39
Long Love, The, 113, 117
Mandala, 144–45
Mother, The, 62–66, 80, 120, 141, 148–49
New Year, The, 142–43, 144, 150
Now and Forever, 77
Other Gods, 98–101, 114, 121, 150
Patriot, The, 94–98, 148–49
Pavilion of Women, 117–21
Promise, The, 110–12, 149
"Revolutionist, The," 30–31
Sons, 43, 50–56, 148–49
This Proud Heart, 77–80, 88, 101
Three Daughters of Madame Liang, The, 143–44
Time Is Noon, The, 137, 139–42, 144, 148–49, 150
Townsman, The, 102–103, 113
Voices in the House, 113, 117
"Will This Earth Hold?" 102

Winds of Heaven, 23
"Woman Who Was Changed, The,"
 147

WORKS: NON-FICTION
American Argument, 152, 153
"America Speaks to China," 102
"Artist in a World of Science, The,"
 152
Bridge for Passing, A, 78, 121
"Child Who Never Grew, The," 135
"Chinese Novel, The," 85-87
Exile, The, 21, 28, 67-71, 72, 75, 76,
 80, 141, 148
Fighting Angel, 67, 71-76, 80, 141, 148
"In China, Too," 22
"In Memoriam: Absalom Syden-
 stricker, 1852-1931," 72, 74
"Is There a Case for Foreign Mis-
 sions?" 48-49
My Several Worlds, 65, 74, 132
Of Men and Women, 92-93
"On the Writing of Novels," 84-85
"Tinder for Tomorrow," 102-103
"What Are We Fighting For in the
 Orient?" 103
"Will This Earth Hold?" 102

Burroughs, Edgar Rice, 87

Canby, Henry Seidel, 38, 75, 83
Cargill, Oscar, 36, 37, 38, 83
Cather, Willa, 116
Chiang Kai-shek, 52, 94-97
Chiang Kai-shek, Madame, 107-108,
 112
Christian Century, The, 47
Chung Yang University, 21
Cornell University, 22
Corrigan, Douglas, 98
Cowie, Alexander, 34
Cowley, Malcolm, 60-61, 83

Dickens, Charles, 18, 22, 40, 115
Dreiser, Theodore, 22, 26, 40, 156n18

East and West Association, 102, 106, 151
Eliot, George, 18
Ellis Island Immigration Center, 133-34

Farewell to Arms, A, 109
Faulkner, William, 65
Faust, 41
Feng Yu Hsiang, 52
Fermi, Enrico, 126
Fitzgerald, Edward, 26
Flowering Judas, The, 51
Forster, E.M., 156
Forum, 22
For Whom the Bell Tolls, 51
Frankfort Academy, 72

Gannett, Lewis, 86
Glasgow, Ellen, 22
Goethe, Johann von, 41
Gordon, Charles, 74
Graves, Robert: *The White Goddess,* 146
Gray, James, 32
Green Hills Farm, 135
Grey, Zane, 86-87

Hardy, Thomas, 149
Harper's, 47
Harris, Theodore, 79, 129, 145, 146
Hemingway, Ernest, 22, 33, 40, 51, 109,
 127
Hocking, W. Ernest, 47, 145, 146
Howe, Edgar Watson, 116
Howells Medal for Distinguished Fic-
 tion, 29
Huckleberry Finn, 18

Index Translationum, 81

Janeway, Elizabeth, 150-51, 166n8
Joyce, James, 149

Kang, Younghill, 42-43, 46, 151
Kiang Kang-Hu, 43-46, 122
King James version of the Bible, 33-34
Kung, Mr., 18, 82

Lagerlof, Selma, 67
La Terre, 38
Laura Messenger Prize, 23
Laymen's Foreign Mission Inquiry, 47-
 49
Leisy, Ernest, 115
Lewis, Sinclair, 22, 42, 82

Lindbergh, Charles, 98
Lin Yutang, 46
Livingstone, David, 74
Look Back in Anger, 153
Lyrical Ballads, 37

Machen, J. Gresham, 49
Mahatma Gandhi Memorial Foundation, 136
Main Street, 42
Manhattan Project, 124–25
Mao Tse-tung, 93, 144
Mencken, H. L., 150
Milton, John: *Paradise Lost*, 121
Min, Queen, 138
Miss Jewell's School, 19
Molière, 40
Muller, Herbert, 152
Muni, Paul 29

Nanking University, 21
Nation, The, 22
National Educational Association, 87
New Republic, 42, 151
New York Times, 43–45, 51, 104, 134
Nixon, President Richard, 15

Oliver Twist, 18
Osborne, John, 153
Osterling, Anders, 80

Paine, Thomas, 152
Pearl S. Buck Foundation, 135, 137, 141
Phelps, William Lyon, 37, 79, 83
Porter, Gene Stratton, 87
Porter, Katherine Anne, 51
Presbyterian Board of Foreign Missions, 49
Pritchett, V. S., 127
Proust, Marcel, 22, 37
Pulitzer Prize, 29, 110

Rainer, Luise, 29
Randolph–Macon Woman's College, 19–20, 84
Rockefeller, John D., 74
Rölvaag, Ole, 35
Romulo, Carlos, 132
Rousseau, Jean Jacques, 152

Rubaiyat of Omar Khayyam, The, 26

Saturday Review of Literature, 83
Scott, Sir Walter, 18
Shakespeare, William, 18
Shanghai Mercury, 18
Shaw, George Bernard, 112
Shui Hu Chuan, 43, 46, 51, 82, 159n31
Snow, Helen F., 151
Southeastern University, 21
Spencer, Cornelia (pseud. of Grace Sydenstricker Yaukey), 20, 51, 87
Spiller's *Literary History of the United States*, 81
Steinbeck, John, 64–65, 81
Story of a Country Town, The, 116
Sun Chuan-fang, 51
Swann's Way, 37
Sydenstricker, Absalom, 16–17, 20, 67–75, 129–31, 140, 148
Sydenstricker, Caroline Stulting, 17–19, 20, 21, 67–74, 129–31, 140, 148
Sydenstricker, Grace, 20, 51, 87

Tarbell, Ida, 71
Thackeray, William Makepeace, 18
Thoreau, Henry David, 22
Tom Sawyer, 18
Training School, The, Vineland, N.J., 135
Ts'ao K'un, 52
Twain, Mark, 81
Tynan, Kenneth, 127
Tzu Hsi, Empress, 130

United China Relief, 102

Van Doren, Carl, 32, 34

Walsh, Richard J., 77, 114, 121, 134, 139, 140, 145, 151
War and Peace, 83
Washington and Lee University, 72
Welcome House, 134–35, 141, 143, 151
White Tiger, 51
Whitman, Walt, 136
Wilder, Thornton, 31, 85
Williams, Dr., 131
Wilson, Edmund, 112

Wilson, Woodrow, 138, 139
Wolfe, Thomas, 78
Woolf, Virginia, 85
Wordsworth, William, 37
Wright, Harold Bell, 87
Wu Pei Fu, 52

Wuthering Heights, 83

Yale Review, 45

Zola, Émile, 22, 38–40, 109